There is a kind of thought that is more or less a representation of what is there, like a map. However, thought has a creative function as well, to create what is there. In fact, almost everything we see around us in the world was created from thought, including all the cities, all the buildings, all the science, all the technology, and almost everything that we call nature. Farmland was produced by thought, by people thinking what they're going to do with the land and then doing it. So without thought we wouldn't have farms; we wouldn't have factories; we wouldn't have ships; we wouldn't have airplanes; we wouldn't have governments. Supposing we have a company like General Motors. People have to think to know what they are supposed to be doing—if they all forgot this, the company would collapse and would cease to exist. So thought can take part in creativity. Thought has created a lot of good things. It is a very powerful instrument, but if we don't notice how it works, it can also do great harm.

Changing Consciousness

Changing Consciousness

Exploring the Hidden Source of the Social, Political, and Environmental Crises Facing Our World

David Bohm
Mark Edwards

HarperSanFrancisco

A Division of HarperCollins*Publishers*

Harper San Francisco and the author, in association with the Rainforest Action Network, will facilitate the planting of two trees for every one tree used in the manufacture of this book.

Designed by Bailey and Kenny.

Photographs by Mark Edwards.

The photograph of a dust storm in Oklahoma on page 33, by Arthur Rothstein, is from *The Depression Years as Photographed by Arthur Rothstein*, 1978, Dover Pictorial Archive Series, Dover Publications, Inc.

Quotations from *Krishnamurti to Himself* (London: Victor Gollancz. Ltd., 1989) are used by permission of the copyright holder: Krishnamurti Foundation Trust Limited, Brockwood Park, Bramdean, Hampshire, U. K.

The photograph on page 92, taken by Mark Edwards, was commissioned by the United Nations Centre for Human Settlements.

FIRST EDITION

Library of Congress Cataloging-in-Publication Data
Bohm, David.
Changing consciousness: exploring the hidden source of the social, political, and environmental crises facing our world / David Bohm and Mark Edwards.—1st ed.
p.   cm.
ISBN 0-06-250072-4
1. Civilization, Modern—1950– . 2. Thought and thinking.
I. Edwards, Mark, 1947– . II. Title.
CB430.B62   1991
909.82—dc20   90-55852
                                                        CIP

91 92 93 94 95 KP 10 9 8 7 6 5 4 3 2 1

Contents

Preface

We would like to begin by giving the reader an idea of how this book came about. We first met in 1983 when Krishnamurti introduced us, on the occasion of being photographed for a book jacket for *The Ending of Time*; however, we had already been interested in what Krishnamurti had to say for a long time. The first of the two of us to discover Krishnamurti was David Bohm, in 1959. And it happened for Mark Edwards in 1966. The course of both our lives was deeply changed by this contact.

For David Bohm, the key effect was to make possible the insight that a wrong functioning of thought is behind most of the troubles of the human race. This insight went along with an understanding of the need for a certain kind of observation of how thought is actually working, whether one is by oneself or taking part in the activities of society.

For Mark Edwards, the key effect was to arouse an intense curiosity to see with his own eyes how the development of civilization has had a wide range of negative consequences, not only in society and in the natural environment, but also in the culture and in the general health of the mind. In his work as a photographer, he verified what Krishnamurti had been saying, and he tried to convey vividly in pictures the destructive effects of the disorder in thought to which Krishnamurti had so passionately called attention.

After the two of us were introduced, we got together from time to time and talked about these issues. Finally we decided to work together to produce a book, in which it was our intention that the photographs and the text combine to give a coherent overall impression of our perceptions of the problems that now threaten the very existence of civilization. This book is the result of our work.

We would like to acknowledge the key contribution of Dr. Patrick de Mare, who introduced one of us (D. B.) to the role of dialogue in the context of what we are talking about in this book. In addition, we wish to thank Sarah Bohm, Mary Cadogan, Derek Edwards, and David Shainberg, all of whom read the manuscript and made helpful comments. Both of us thank Sarah Bohm for constant encouragement and support.

January 1990

Introduction

This book opens up an inquiry into the human condition at a particularly crucial period in history. An immense and ever accelerating technological development has in principle brought about enormous new possibilities for a creative and happy life. But at the same time this development is threatening our civilization, and indeed, perhaps the human race and our planet itself, with almost total destruction. This book is aimed at making more than a mere comment on the present state of affairs. Its purpose is to sketch out the deeper causes underlying this environmental, social, and cultural crisis and to indicate further lines of inquiry that could perhaps lead to its resolution.

The book consists of two parts. In the first part is a picture essay by Mark Edwards that brings out vividly the worldwide nature of the crisis. The exploration by David Bohm of the deeper causes of the crisis begins in chapter 1 with a discussion between him and Mark Edwards in response to this essay. In chapter 2, the connection between the technological and the psychological development of humanity is examined, and this is again illustrated by photographs that convey the social and material conditions in societies at different stages of development. These include photographs of a Stone Age tribe in the South American jungle; peasant farmers in South Asia and Africa enclosed in a medieval way of life; adults and children caught up in a fight for survival in the industrial revolution taking place in some of the newly developing nations; and the complex life of people in some of the most technologically advanced communities in Europe and America. As well as showing something significant of the daily lives of a whole cross section of our race, Mark Edwards's photographs bring out the environmental problems that result, inevitably, from the patterns of daily living that threaten to destroy our future. The photographs also show the fundamental similarity of human beings irrespective of the technological age to which they belong.

People are similar not only in their basic drives and urges but also in their fear and anxiety, which has increased along with the growth of technology. A resulting general disturbance of the order of operation of the brain and mind contributes in a basic way to the general crisis that we are discussing. It is this theme that is taken up by David Bohm in the second part of the book. The text begins by calling attention to how the current crisis is constantly sustained and exacerbated by a basic and pervasive disharmony between the intellect and emotions that has been increasing since very early times. This disharmony is mirrored in our personal relationships, in relationships between governments, and in our relationship with nature. In large part because of this disharmony, many of us in the modern world have felt a sense of loss, of missing something, in spite of our great technological gains, which should have made us feel that life has been enriched rather than impoverished.

Indeed, for both the rich and the poor, life is dominated by an ever growing current of problems, most of which seem to have no real and lasting solution. Clearly we have not touched the deeper causes of our troubles. It is the main point of this book that the ultimate source of all these problems is in thought itself, the very thing of which our civilization is most proud, and therefore the one thing that is "hidden" because of our failure seriously to engage with its actual working in our own individual lives and in the life of society. This engagement is carried out in some depth in the text. In the exchange between David Bohm and Mark Edwards, readers are invited, as it were, to join in the inquiry and to go on with it, not only by themselves but also with others who may be interested. If such work is carried further, it could give rise to a fundamental change of consciousness itself, giving rise to a more harmonious way of life.

Part

I

THOUGHT AND THE HUMAN CONDITION

Child with toy gun, Bucharest, Romania.

A man carries his wife, suffering from cholera, away from fighting during the Bangladesh war, 1971.

Chapter 1

THE WORLD CRISIS AND THOUGHT

MARK
EDWARDS:

Having traveled quite extensively, I feel on the basis of what I have seen that a new approach to living is urgently needed. As I have already pointed out in the introduction, our problems, both personal and collective, do not generally yield to our present way of thinking. I'd like to start our dialogue by showing you a selection of photographs I have taken that focus attention on the disorder in the present state of society.

Almost the first thing you are taught in school is that the world is divided into nations. It's presented to the child as if it were a law of nature. As you grow up you start to see how costly these national boundaries are. Governments throughout the world spend billions of dollars on defense, and sooner or later there is war and terrible suffering. Countless numbers of people have killed or been killed or made homeless, like the people in the photograph — an endless panorama of horror in the name of security. These are the obvious effects of nationalism, and later we could perhaps look at the more subtle consequences. Let's start by examining this tendency we have to divide things up and in this way to produce conflict.

DAVID
BOHM:

This tendency to produce conflict has come from our thought, from how it has evolved over the whole period of civilization. Thought has developed in such a way that it has an intrinsic disposition to divide things up. We do, of course, divide things up properly and usefully, for example, distinguishing between various kinds of nutritious plants or between sheep and goats, and so on. There are all sorts of legitimate ways of making such distinctions and divisions. But we then carry it too far, and we don't notice what we're doing. Thus, we also divide between nations. But there's a big difference when it comes to saying, for example, that I'm now sitting here on a chair, while over there is a table. They are really separate things and not significantly connected. So I can say that they are different from each other, in the sense that I can move one of these objects independently of the other. But if I say that one side of the table is different from the other, this won't work, because if I push on one side, then the other also moves. Now, people tend to think that the distinction between nations is like the distinction between the chair and the table. But these latter are really quite independent objects, and nations are not.

This distinction has been determined by thought. Every nation has come into existence through some thought that said, "We exist; we declare that we exist; we have our independence," or else it gradually came to that. Thus, we now have a lot of nations that never existed before—a hundred years ago who would have thought of Zimbabwe? Kampuchea? Bangladesh? And yet people are supposed to die for nations, and give up all their possessions for them, and put their children into the army for them, and, as is shown in the photograph, sacrifice everything for them. They seem to be supremely precious realities—as you say, the world as a whole is ready to pay a thousand billion dollars a year to defend these nations. Nevertheless, they are created by thinking, although people seem to forget this. The boundaries between nations are created entirely by thinking. As you cross the boundary there is no physical change, and very often the people are not all that different. The difference is entirely due to differences in custom and habit and history that began by their thinking differently. They gradually came to have different languages and to have somewhat different ways of life. Then they said, "Here we have a nation," and they thought, "We're all united within our nation—we're different from all the other nations."

Of course, nations may serve a useful purpose as convenient administrative units, and these may correspond to groups of people with a fairly common culture as well as other common interests. But the importance of the differences between nations has always been enormously exaggerated. Indeed, different nations are fairly closely connected physically, and now in the modern world the connection is much closer. Economi-

A mother gives her child a
spoonful of milk, Denmark.

A mother gives her child a saucer
of milk while her mother-in-law
spins cotton, Chhattera village,
India.

cally we all depend on one another, and ecologically we're seeing that, with the change of climate and for other reasons, we will all suffer together when things go wrong. So there are a great many key points at which we are intimately bound together. The idea of national sovereignty denies this and says that each nation can do what it likes. This would only make sense if the nations really were independent of each other. But people are overlooking our interdependence and saying that no one can tell our nation what to do. Yet, for example, in Brazil they are cutting down and burning the rain forests. Some of the Brazilian politicians are saying with resentment that you northern, prosperous people are producing most of the carbon dioxide and you are then blaming us for changing the climate. Who do you think you are to tell us what to do with our Amazon? And we in the north similarly say, who do you in Brazil think you are to tell us what to do with our industries? But talking this way, how can we ever get together to stop all this destructive activity?

This way of thinking has been given a name: *fragmentation*. The word *fragment* means to smash, to break up. It doesn't mean to divide. The parts of a watch could be divided, but they could still make up the whole. However, if you smashed the watch, you would get fragments, parts just arbitrarily broken up. People tend to think of nations as parts, but they are really fragments. If you try to take out one nation from the whole context, trade and all sorts of other connections would be broken. Moreover, people pretend that their nation is more united than it actually is. There are all sorts of divisions within each nation that are often far worse than those between nations.

Fragmentation consists of false division, making a division where there is a tight connection, and also false unification, uniting where there is not unity. For example, I say there is no nation that is really united. There is tremendous conflict within each nation — between the poor and the rich, between the bureaucracy and the rest of the people, between one ethnic group and another. So it is a fiction that any nation is united and that one nation is sharply distinct from another. And evidently, if we try to live by fiction, we are going to get into trouble. So it is this fragmentation, this fictional way of thinking, that has created all this trouble and produced the armies and the nuclear bombs and the refugees with all their suffering and also our inability to solve the ecological problems, and economic problems, and so on.

Tuareg nomads with umbrellas
and a radio cassette player,
Niger.

A boy talks to his friend using
a walkie-talkie, Denmark.

ME: I think that it is difficult to see that thought can create what appear to be independently real things, things like these divisions. Thought tends to assume that it is only reflecting what is actually there, not producing what is there.

DB: Yes. Of course, there is a kind of thought that is more or less a representation of what is there, like a map. However, thought has a creative function as well, to create what is there. In fact, almost everything we see around us in the world was created from thought, including all the cities, all the buildings, all the science, all the technology, and almost everything that we call nature. Farmland was produced by thought, by people thinking what they're going to do with the land and then doing it. So without thought we wouldn't have farms; we wouldn't have factories; we wouldn't have ships; we wouldn't have airplanes; we wouldn't have governments. Supposing we have a company like General Motors. People have to think to know what they are supposed to be doing—if they all forgot this, the company would collapse and would cease to exist. So thought can take part in creativity. Thought has created a lot of good things. It is a very powerful instrument, but if we don't notice how it works, it can also do great harm.

ME: Would you define what you mean by thought? Then we could perhaps consider how it works.

DB: This is a very complex and subtle question, but I'll begin by talking around the subject for a while.

First of all, thought is involved in expressing, applying, and creating knowledge. In order to express and apply knowledge you must think, and in order to create knowledge you must think. So you have to connect thought with knowledge. Without knowledge we would not really be human. And there is so much knowledge of all kinds—some of it is false or misleading, and some is correct and useful.

What is knowledge? This is really a key question. First of all, we have practical knowledge, like knowledge of how to ride a bicycle. We can't really say exactly what that is. It's tacit; it is a skill that we build up by experience. Then we begin to distinguish, for example, between sheep and goats, probably with hardly any thinking, just by experience, especially under primitive conditions. Probably people in such conditions did very little thinking as we know it, but they were building up knowledge by long tradition and practice. And then we begin to think about that knowledge and make it more systematic and orderly. In doing this, we give names. Each name determines a category of a general kind, such as sheep and goats, men and women, knives and forks. Such names are evidently necessary for useful purposes. As I have just said, each name of this kind represents a general class of things (whereas the name of a person represents only that individual). Once you name something you are able to call it up in your mind, along with the image of it and the utility of it — what you can do with it. You can begin to work with it and share it with other people, as it becomes communicable.

You can then begin to use thought in order to solve problems in your mind without actually having to solve them first in reality. There was a well-known psychologist, Jean Piaget, who investigated the development of thought in young children. He cites the case of such a child at the stage just before he could solve a problem in his mind. The little boy saw a coin in a half-open matchbox, and he wanted to open the box and get it out. What he did first was open his mouth and pretend to pull something out, and then he did it with the matchbox. So he was using his mouth to represent the matchbox. Later, you don't need your mouth; you have an image in your mind. So the child is then able to open the box in the mental image and pull out the coin, and in this way he knows what to do. He thus begins to solve problems in his mind.

Even chimpanzees can do this to a small extent — they can see the possibility of putting sticks together to reach fruit. We have much bigger brains and so can do it much better. And we also have language and can therefore communicate about it. In addition, we have the opposable thumb and forefinger, which is very important to carrying out the implications of thought in an exact way. The dolphin's brain and the whale's are bigger than ours. They may be as intelligent as we are, but what they lack is the opposable thumb and forefinger. We may be led to think that they are not all that intelligent. But in some ways you could say they are more intelligent, because they don't fight each other; they live fairly happily; and you see them enjoying themselves much of the time.

ME: They live without nationalism!

DB: They don't seem to fight each other for food or anything — except for us they would have no serious problems. They have been here for twenty million years apparently and in themselves are quite successful species. With all our possibilities, we are in a different category, however. But such possibilities are also very dangerous. They threaten the existence of our species, or even of the whole world of nature.

ME: Some of the environmentalists are pointing out that nationalism makes it very difficult to solve the world's environmental problems. And they feel that nationalism in some magical way will lose its hold on people. I can't see that happening without a sustained inquiry into the process of thought that has produced nationalism—in fact, the reverse seems more likely, especially if conditions get worse along lines that are predicted, for example, climate changes due to the greenhouse effect.

DB: What we must do first is understand the source, otherwise what one says about ending nationalism may be just a vain hope. People in the Middle Ages hoped that the plague would go away, but they didn't realize that it was carried by fleas, which in turn were carried by rats, which were carried by ships from one country to another. They didn't think about the fleas and the rats and the ships. Later people saw the rats coming out of the ships, and they knew they were carrying fleas and realized the connection between fleas and plague and on the ropes holding the ships they built plates so that rats couldn't come ashore. That was a big step in stopping the plague, because they'd learned how it was carried. So if nationalism is the plague, we have to understand the origin of that plague.

ME: Nationalism looks to me like a kind of tribalism amplified in the modern age with the aid of the communications industry. This way of thinking is interfering with the intelligence needed to see where division is appropriate and where it is not.

DB: It is basically this sort of thought that lacks the necessary intelligence. To meet this challenge, we have to begin by examining the general nature of thought. To begin with, we can say that thought is knowledge that is being applied to a particular case or that is being created by thinking about things. You begin to think, What shall I do? What's this all about? What you think then goes into the memory; it becomes a kind of program. In thinking something, it becomes thought—the language says so. The word *thinking* means something active is going on; the word *thought* means it has gone on. You usually think that thought has gone and therefore has no effect. But thought has actually gone into the program, into the memory. It's not really just the memory of what has happened, but also of what to do, of what to believe, of how things should be divided up or united, of who you are, of what you belong to, and all that. Now, when this memory works, it doesn't come back as thinking; it works almost immediately, without thinking, through the way you respond, through its effect on how you see things, and so on.

ME: It feels, as we said earlier, like a law of nature. We have been conditioned in this way since childhood.

DB: Young children never know that one nation is different from another until they're told. But when they're told by people whom they believe — their parents or whoever it is — they think, Well, now we know. And when they know, they don't have to think anymore. It is thought that now works and, for example, makes them feel uneasy with a foreign person. Thought affects the body, creating the stance of being cautious. And the adrenaline flows, because there is a certain amount of fear and mistrust, not quite the sense of ease you have with someone you know. Thought works in this way for all sorts of things. Thus, if you want to drive a car, you have to be told all sorts of things; you have to learn how. But when you drive, it's no use unless you act without thinking. If you had to think before applying what you've learned, it would be too late. The same kind of thought that enables you to drive a car operates when you become hostile to someone of another group, whether it be a different race, nation, or religion.

Suppose you have two religions. Thought defines religion — the thought about the nature of God and various questions like that. Such thought is very important because it is about God, who is supposed to be supreme. The thought about what is of supreme value must have the highest force. So if you disagree about that, the emotional impact can be very great, and you will then have no way to settle it. Two different beliefs about God will thus produce intense fragmentation — similarly with thoughts about the nature of society, which is also very important, or with ideologies such as communism and capitalism, or with different beliefs about your family or about your money. Whatever it is that is very important to you, fragmentation in your thought about it is going to be very powerful in its effects.

ME: Yes, and politicians are particularly adroit at manipulating this tendency to fragmentary thinking in the form of nationalism. In fact, their careers depend on it.

DB: Well, they think about it all the time, and it's now in their thought. People accept it as a matter of course that they can't trust people in another country. And when they think about it, they see that equally one can't trust the people in their own country. Fundamentally the people in one's own country are no more trustworthy than they are anywhere else — every politician knows that.

ME: There are some divisions that appear to be more real than national boundaries — the Asiatic world, with its religious traditions, and the industrialized world, with its materialistic traditions emphasizing technology. However, in the long run, the differences may not be so great. The industrial world is poisoning the entire planet with chemical pollution, and in the Third World more and more land is being destroyed by deforestation and overpopulation caused mainly by poverty. I don't think that people are particularly happy or fulfilled in either culture. In the East people think that if they had our riches and security they'd be happy beyond measure; in the West we feel that we have lost something that they still have in the East. If we had a simpler life, closer to nature, we suppose, we would be at peace. (The rich have always romanticized poverty.) Can we examine this difference between the Asiatic world and the industrialized world in the light of what you have just said?

DB: First of all, this division arises out of the way people historically have thought differently in the Asiatic and the Western worlds. In the Western world thought has turned toward science and technology. Some historians, such as Joseph Needham, have asked why the Chinese didn't develop technology though they had a higher civilization than Europe had in the Middle Ages. He gave several explanations — we don't need to go into them in detail here. But for various reasons Western thought has turned toward technology and industrial development, perhaps partly because of its early emphasis on the concept of measure, which goes back to ancient Greece and even before. By contrast, partly because of the kind of philosophy that prevailed in the East, which put the immeasurable into first place, Eastern thought has been more static in

Women perform *puja* in the
Hooghly River, Calcutta.

Woman walking past an
abandoned model airplane,
New York.

its treatment of the domain of the measurable, and so people there have been more satisfied to stay with things as they are. But ultimately this difference is due to thought. It seems very unlikely that it is due to race; in many ways, the Japanese are doing better at certain key aspects of our Western thought than we are. I'm sure the Chinese are going to do well too once they get going, because they work very hard.

So there isn't any intrinsic distinction between Eastern and Western humanity that I can see operating. Differences exist because thought develops like a stream that happens to go one way here and another way there. Once it develops it produces real physical results that people are looking at, but they don't see where these results are coming from — that's one of the basic features of fragmentation. When they have produced these divisions they see that real things have happened, so they'll start with these real things as if they just suddenly got there by themselves, or evolved in nature by themselves. That's the second mistake that thought makes. It produces a result, and then it says, I didn't do it; it's there by itself, and I must correct it. But if thought is constantly making this result and then saying, I've got to stop it, this is absurd. Because thought is caught up in this absurdity, it is producing all sorts of negative consequences, then treating them as independent and saying, I must stop them. It is as if a man with his right hand were doing things he didn't want to do, and with the left hand he tried to hold back his right hand. All he has to do is to stop the whole process, and then he doesn't have that problem.

ME: For most of us, it is very unusual for thought to pause in the way you suggest. It just seems to keep going of its own accord.

DB: That's the third feature of thought; it seems to have some inertia, a tendency to continue. It seems to have a necessity that we keep on doing it. Is there actually such a necessity? This is crucial. The fact is, thought is producing crazy things like fragmentation. It's doing something insane, such as producing something and then saying that it didn't do it, that it happened independently. And then it says, I can't stop it, even though I can see that it makes no sense, because I feel the necessity of going on with it.

The word *necessary* means that it cannot be otherwise. This means we believe that there is no other way. But in addition it has a root that is significant; this is the Latin *ne cesse*, which means "don't yield."

Intellectually it comes out as something that cannot be otherwise, and emotionally as something that doesn't yield. This latter implies a disposition to hold and not to give up readily. Of course, there are many occasions on which such a disposition may be appropriate. Nevertheless, we also need to be able to let go of this sort of attitude when we see evidence that it is not called for. However (as in the case of the necessity to keep on thinking certain thoughts when to do so makes no sense), we often find that we cannot easily give up the tendency to hold rigidly to patterns of thought built up over a long time. We are then caught up in what may be called absolute necessity. This kind of thought leaves no room at all intellectually for any other possibility, while emotionally and physically, it means we take a stance in our feelings, in our bodies, and, indeed, in our whole culture, of holding back or resisting. This stance implies that under no circumstances whatsoever can we allow ourselves to give up certain things or change them.

ME: Yes, even children get set in their ways. Older people become skilled at defending narrower and narrower points of view, and that seems so lacking in intelligence. I would really like to explore this tendency with you.

DB: We shall have to discuss this later, when we go into more generally the relationship between intellect and emotions.

ME: As society is organized at present, it seems impossible to satisfy basic needs for everyone. More and more people throughout the world are homeless. They suffer terribly. When we talk about the Third World, we should include those who are poor wherever they are — even if they are living in the West. In the same way, I regard rich and middle-class people with access to sophisticated technology as being in the industrialized world, even if they live in developing countries.

The rich world responds to the problems in the Third World by creating more and more specialized organizations. One deals with water and sanitation, another with shelter, another with food and education, another with population, and so on. So again we see this tendency to separate things into compartments. If there were a real dialogue between these groups, a great deal more could be achieved in practical terms. This fragmented way of thinking prevents a deeper inquiry into our problems by concentrating on effects. All our energy is taken up with

A homeless woman and her son living in concrete sewage pipes on a building site, Calcutta.

Homeless men and women living under Waterloo Bridge, London.

our response to the immediate issues, and we don't get into contact with the whole problem.

DB: Yes, we've touched on that by saying that thought creates a problem and then creates a separate approach in trying to solve it. This doesn't get to the root of the real problem, because the root is the overall process of thought itself. It's like the old Sufi story of the man who lost the key to his house. He was found to be looking for it under a light. He looked and looked and couldn't find it. Finally someone asked where he had lost the key. He answered, "Well, I did in fact lose it over there." And when asked why he didn't look for it over there, he said, "Well, it's dark over there, but there is light here for me to look."

ME: What is it that would look at thought?

DB: This is a very subtle question. Let me begin by pointing out that the most fundamental characteristic of the word *thought* is that it is in the past tense. It is what has been thought, though it's still not gone. One of the common beliefs is that thought, when you've finished with it, has gone. But we've said that it is actually there, as if it were on a computer disk. The computer disk not only repeats all sorts of facts, but, even more important, it actually operates the computer in a certain way. That way has to be changed from time to time because things change. Or as Krishnamurti put it, thought and knowledge are limited. They cannot cover everything, if only because they are based on things that have happened in the past, whereas everything changes. However, one of the most common assumptions of thought is that thought is not limited.

ME: Most of us would see that thought is limited by experience and in its own way reflects experience.

DB: Thought is not just reflecting whatever is there, but on the basis of what is known from the past, it helps to create the impression of what is there. It selects; it abstracts; and in doing this, it chooses certain aspects, which then attract our attention. But what is there is immensely beyond what thought can thus grasp. As an analogy, let us consider a map: a map does not correspond with a territory in a direct and immediately perceptible way; it's only in some very abstract sense that it corresponds. For example, if you have a division between one country and another, there's a line on the map — that's an abstraction. And there's another line that is supposed to be somewhere in between the two countries—that's another abstraction. So there's a correspondence of these two abstractions. In this way, the map may enable you to see certain abstract relationships that could help guide you in the territory. But the map is much, much less than the territory, and it's not always even right.

Thought could be regarded as a more abstract and generalized kind of map of reality. (That's one way of looking at it, though there are other ways.) Clearly it needs constant improvement with change, as new maps are needed in different areas. Thus if you use the Mercator projection near the equator, it's fairly accurate. But if you use it near the poles, it's wrong, because, for example, it would imply that northern Greenland is infinite. Nevertheless, when you got there you would find that it's not that way. So maps may be wrong in structure. Moreover, as I've already said, they're always incomplete, because there is always much more in the territory than there could be on the map. Similarly, thought cannot be complete, and therefore it requires constant perception of that fact. It can be a guide, but it can do this only if you also look at the fact, at the territory.

ME: The difficulty here is to distinguish perception of the fact from the thought.

DB: That's right. That's one of the problems, that thought affects the way you see the fact and affects the way you see the territory. For example, when you cross from one country to another, you see another nation, but really, where is it? It's not there by itself; it's only there because you think it's there or because of what people have done because they think it's there. Therefore, thought is not keeping track of its own consequences, of its own activity. You need some sort of process of perception to keep track of that. You cannot by thinking alone look at the territory.

ME: You're pointing out that perception and thought are different, but I feel it is important to test this for oneself. When you look at something, especially something you are not familiar with, there is perception, but it is followed very rapidly by thought. There may be only a fraction of a second of delay, for example, on perceiving a face and having an opinion about it (beautiful or ugly), but with attention it is possible to sense this difference. Perception feels quite different from the thought about the thing you have been looking at.

18

DB: Thought is conditioned to react somewhat as if it were a computer disk and can therefore respond extremely rapidly. It is helpful to regard thought as acting basically like a conditioned reflex. It takes time to build up the memory-based reactions, but once this is done the responses are so fast that it is difficult to see their mechanical nature. For example, if you look at a tree, you'll immediately say the word *tree* rather as a disk on a computer set up to recognize the shape of a tree might do. All the information and general responses connected with this word are then called up automatically.

But reactive thought and perception of an actual fact are very different. The first point to notice is that we are able to perceive an actual fact through our senses. Everybody can see that we can perceive this through our senses, whether it be our eyes or our ears or our sense of touch, and that in this way we get information that thought cannot possibly supply. The least we can say, therefore, is that we have a combination of sense perception and thought.

The second point, however, is that there is yet another kind of perception: perception through the mind. With this, we can perceive whether our thought is coherent or not. For example, you may be in conflict with another person and your thought may lead you automatically to blame that person, thus pushing the blame away from yourself and making yourself feel better. However, perhaps in a quieter moment, you may have an indefinable sense intimating that you are at least in part responsible for the problem. This is a feeling that to attribute the sole cause of the trouble to the other person is not consistent with subtler aspects of the whole fact, of which you have started to become aware. As a result, you may be led to question the immediate response of your thought, which is set to try to blame the other person and thus obtain relief.

I think that when this happens, we begin to go a bit beyond thought. Indeed, thought stops for a moment. In some sense we are then perceiving, but not through the senses; we are looking through the mind. Such perception, in which one goes deeply into the more subtle aspects of incoherence, can invalidate a false program so that subsequent thought can be free from it and therefore more coherent.

To sum up, then, thought is a response based on memory, but as one can discover by actual experience in the way that has just been described, it can be affected by perception, both through the senses and through

19

Howrah Bridge, Calcutta,
photographed after the rush hour.

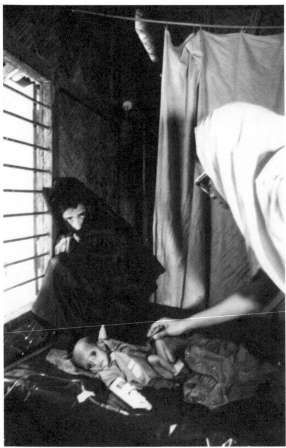

Child being treated for
dysentery in a village hospital,
Bangladesh. More and more
children, like the one in this
photograph, survive childhood
illness.

the mind, and this is evidently not based primarily on memory. Through such perception, we can see the incoherence in our thought (for example, we can detect fragmentation). We can then go on to perceiving new ways of making distinctions and new relationships among the things thus distinguished that were more congruent with actual fact.

I suggest that this approach can be carried further to make possible new discoveries, new ideas, and new insights. All this indicates some faculty that goes beyond memory, that is not just sense perception. This is something we will explore in more detail later on, because it is of fundamental significance.

ME: Yes. Perhaps we can begin by exploring the incoherence of thought in a more concrete way by considering the question of overpopulation. Look at this bridge across the Hooghly River in Calcutta. (I especially avoided photographing it during the rush hour!) This problem is not only present in the underdeveloped countries. In the West, the population is already so large that, with our much greater access to goods and services, with the attendant use of natural resources, we are making a correspondingly destructive impact on nature. If the Third World caught up with our standard of living, it would be the end of nature and us. For example, someone worked out that if everyone in China and India used toilet paper, every tree in the world would be gone in a year.

The rapid increase of population in the Third World is in large measure a result of people's continuing their traditional ways of thinking under conditions in which modern medicine preserves life. Thus, in olden times it was a tradition to have eight or more births, and these children were thought of as a gift from God. Many children died in their first years, but nowadays the very successful campaigns to inoculate children against common diseases, the treatment of dysentery and malaria, and perhaps other factors have kept many alive who would have died. But the intervention of technology did not greatly change attitudes about family life. It seems that people are, in effect, programmed so that they often prefer to adapt to terrible conditions rather than question traditional values, such as those implying the need for as many children as possible. These values seem to have great importance, even if they are not appropriate under the new conditions with which we are now faced.

DB: You've just called them traditional *values*, and the question is clearly concerned essentially with what we value. Values may be affected by thought, but values in themselves go beyond thought. What we value is what moves us. Thus, if you see a jewel on the ground, you may sense that it has value—it excites you. You can then pick it up, but if you see that it is synthetic, you don't take it very seriously, even though it may be little different from a natural jewel. In this way, it is clear that value moves you.

This is interesting, because the root of the word *value* is the same as that of *valor* and *valient*; it means "strength." You could say that in primitive times people *felt* values, *perceived* values (without words), by the fact that they were strongly moved. Later they were able to put a word to it and describe that fact, and eventually the word began to move them in a way similar to the original perception. Thus tradition contains a programmed set of values based on thought and words and on past experiences of value carried along in such thought and words and memory. It can therefore react just like any other thought, practically immediately, without thinking. So you *sense* the value that is in your tradition. That is to say, you don't stop to think about it; you *feel* it as immediately given. If you feel value in this way, you want to hold on to it.

It is hard to question such values, partly because of the traditional sharp distinction between thought and feeling. Traditionally, one says that if it's a feeling in the gut, it's not a thought. The feeling is *me*. This is regarded as a true perception and therefore something that is not really open to question, though one admits that a thought is something that could perhaps be questioned. Traditional thought thus implies the necessity of always acting according to such feelings, even though they are the result of the programming. And as tradition grows, with constant accretion of memories of experiences along with those of verbal teachings, it tends to build up to a notion of absolute necessity. In the way I described earlier, this gives rise to a compulsive urge not to yield under any circumstances whatsoever, to hold rigidly to the entire structure at all costs.

It is clear, then, that thoughts and feelings are weaving together in a very closely connected way. But people do not perceive this process. Or at best, they are only dimly aware of it. But for the most part, it just works.

At some stage people may nevertheless begin to question tradition. But it's hard not only for the reasons I've already given, but because there are also objective factors in the content of thought that make it difficult. For example, in the past, only a few children would survive, so that you actually had to have a lot of them to make up for this. And also, especially in certain parts of the world, you still need children to take care of you when you get older, because society is organized that way. So, at least in the limited context of your own circle, it may look very rational to have more children.

In addition, all societies, especially those of the West, have become so fragmented and mechanical that it often seems that there is little meaning to life, that there are just people doing their own dreary jobs. People are therefore not much related and feel that they have very little significance, very little value, not much of a purpose in life. Then they may say that the family seems to be the only place where they could be meaningfully related. But the main purpose of the family is to have children. Without children, the family would seem to have no purpose, and so it would lose its meaning. People may therefore have children just to provide some meaning to their lives. Moreover, many women say that they are built to have children, and that if they don't have them there is something missing. There are all sorts of thoughts of that nature. Whether they are correct or not, we have to investigate. But on the face of it, they may seem to be fairly reasonable. For example, families in the West are now generally too small and impermanent for the proper raising of children, but people don't see any other possibility. Nevertheless, people are faced with the decision of what they are going to do with their lives, and most of them are led to say that they are going to get married and have a family, even if it is not of the right size or degree of stability for the psychological needs of children.

But then, if they have a large family, there is yet another problem: poverty and overcrowding (which the picture shows) and no way of taking care of children properly. Even in the West, there is a great deal of such poverty. To deal with this, some people suggest birth control as a means of limiting population and abortion as a way of not having unwanted children who will not be taken care of properly. But others say that birth control is immoral and that the fetus has an absolute right to live. When these two sides try to talk to each other, they can't. That they cannot talk, not only on this question but also on a vast range of other fundamental problems, is much more serious than the issues dividing them. What happens then is that people give up trying to talk to each other seriously. In this way we each as individuals are eventually left with taking on only the responsibility to take care of ourselves and those immediately around us as best we can, and we conclude that we can do nothing about the rest. Either we are not interested, or else we say, "What can I do?"

All this is thought. It adds up to the conclusion that nothing fundamental can be done. Things just go on in the old way, with superficial changes. The population increases relentlessly. To add to this, some religions have come up with thoughts further supporting the notion that it is wrong to interfere with producing children, and even now some of them are saying this. What they say or imply is that God wants more children. But people won't look at the simple fact of arithmetic that if the population increases at 2.5 percent per year (which is not far from what it's actually doing in some countries), it will increase ten times in a hundred years, ten thousand million times in a thousand years. There will then be a trillion people per square mile of the earth's habitable surface. In seven thousand years, the population will increase beyond the mass of the known universe! People haven't thought about this, and if they did they would see that there must be something absurd in saying that God wants people to produce children at this rate of increase. God must also have it in mind to stop it at some point or other. I remember reading about a conference of people from the East in India where they were talking about population, and they said, "Well, don't worry, God will send plagues and wars to limit the population."

ME: In a way God has, because he's sent dysentery, for example, which is a tremendous killer of children! But thought invents medicines to cure such diseases. AIDS seems to be the response of a more modern kind of God. But perhaps that too will yield to science, and, of course, we all hope it will.

DB: But the trouble with this way of thinking is that we've got in the way of God's will with our medical skill. Some people used to warn, Don't interfere with God's will. And in a certain sense it could be said that they were right. For, if you bring in more medical care, you'll make another problem.

24

I would rather say, however, that we are not looking at the whole problem. Thought is fragmentary — it thinks about this disease and attacks just this one thing; it doesn't think about the broader issue of what is going to happen afterward. It is actually all interconnected, what's going to happen all around. To ignore this is more fragmentation. We solve the medical problem, but in doing that, we don't think of the population problem, the carbon dioxide problem, the forest problem, the overcrowding problem, and so on. When we finally do get around to thinking of these, we treat them separately.

ME: We keep coming back to this point that complex technology requires the exercise of a greater intelligence — a different way of thinking — if each new development is not to create more problems. However, some people might say that it is easy for us to discuss these problems from a distance, but how is all this going to affect the people walking over that bridge, and what relevance does this have, and how can solutions evolve from a way of looking at thought?

DB: If I'm right in saying that thought is the ultimate origin or source, it follows that if we don't do anything about thought, we won't get anywhere. We may momentarily relieve the population problem, the ecological problem, and so on, but they will come back in another way. So I'm saying that we have got to examine this question of thought.

Now, how can you influence all these people? Well, you've got to begin with those who can listen, because everything new started with a few people. At the time of Newton, for example, there were not a hundred scientists of any merit in Europe. They could have said, "Look at this vast mass of ignorant people, going around just living their lives." Nevertheless, science had a tremendous effect, though not all to the good. But still, it shows that small things can have big effects — one small thing being, for example, more and more people understanding that something has to happen. Thus, we already see the Green movement growing. They are doing good work, and I think that much more should be done along these lines. But the important point is that they're not considering thought. That is to say, they are not considering the fundamental cause, just the effect.

ME: Human activity guided by thought is destroying the balance of nature. The rain forests in South America and the Far East are being cut down

Burning the Amazon rain forest.

Woman eating a hot dog by a fountain, New York.

partly by land speculators, partly to repay the foreign debt, partly by cattle ranchers, and partly by migrants from overcrowded cities. In the 1960s the military government in Brazil called the Amazon "a land without people for people without land." Cattle ranches are now carved out of the wilderness not only to supply beef within Brazil, but also to grow soybeans that are exported and fed to cattle to produce cheap hamburger meat abroad. Within a few years this land that was a forest for millions of years generally turns to wasteland. The release of carbon dioxide from burning the wood adds to the industrial emissions from the West that are changing the climate. The world is threatened with rising sea levels, ozone depletion, acid rain, and desertification. The evidence makes it look very likely that we are on the edge of a precipice that, as you have pointed out, thought has unintentionally created. In the long run it seems unlikely that civilization can survive, unless cooperation on a level never seen before can develop. Our attachment to our programs about what is necessary prevents this. I have seen how much suffering people are prepared to put up with in order to defend such ideas. They are ready to endure terrible poverty, wars, and unhappiness beyond measure in order to sustain their customary ways of thinking. Do you think that this is because it is not apparent that that thought has produced these effects, that we are blind to how thought is producing them?

DB: That's an important point. I think that to a certain extent people are failing to see what thought is doing because they haven't paid any serious attention to these questions before. Moreover, thought has a general tendency to defend itself against evidence of its falseness, especially when its basic values are questioned. This is in part because, as I said earlier, thought produces all sorts of things, treats them as independent of thought and as being of such a high value that they are regarded as absolutely necessary. The tendency is then to defend whatever has been given so high a value. Thus, thought creates the nation, saying that it has this sort of value, and this gives rise to a feeling that means that I must defend it at all costs. That feeling includes the notion that I must keep on thinking that it has a high value; otherwise, I can't continue to defend it. In this way you begin to feel the absolute necessity to hold to these thoughts. Especially in times of war people do that. There is censorship, requiring that we must have a special government department to give us false news so that we will be able to hold to the encouraging thought that our armies are doing well and the government is really in command of the situation.

ME: Over and over again I hear journalists, editors, and television producers say that we must publish or broadcast environmental stories that give people hope. "There has been too much bad news; everyone is tired of it." They go from one extreme to the other to keep people interested. The question is, Why don't we emphasize instead the need to value the earth, the air, the rivers, the sea, on which we depend totally for our lives? We seem to love our technology much more.

DB: Well, that's the result of our whole history. Early primitive peoples did place a very high value on the earth. I've read about certain tribes of South American Indians who thought of the earth as their mother and believed that they must take care of their mother. But now there is a relatively new view that the earth is something to be exploited. Some people blame this on the Judeo-Christian tradition, which says that God told us to multiply and to use everything for our own advantage. But I don't think that is the whole story. For example, the ancient Romans, who were not highly influenced by the Judeo-Christian tradition, created vast deserts, though they still had remnants of belief in the earth goddesses. The older earth religions had degenerated and become corrupt by that time. Somehow the development of civilization itself corrupted the whole relationship and led people to think about nature as something to be exploited. There seems to be a deeper tendency in civilized life to produce such thoughts that are very destructive in their ultimate implications.

ME: I was in Denmark recently, and the Danes told me that their first environmental disaster occurred during the Iron Age when people cut down all the trees. They suddenly had iron tools, enabling them to cut down trees very effectively, which had very serious consequences even at that time. The scale of destruction now is unimaginable, but we still feel that we are so small and the sky and the planet so vast that we cannot fully accept the fact that our actions can significantly affect the climate.

DB: There is some tendency when one has the technical ability just to do whatever is possible without thinking about whether it will be an advantage in the long run. In your pictures, it seems to be implied that if people can cut down forests and make a bit of money, they somehow can't refrain, even though it is fairly clear that rather trivial gains are made compared with what is lost. If you look at the picture, you can't help thinking that many of these people would be better off if they never had these cheap hamburgers. They'd be more healthy.

ME: This is how Christopher Columbus described the island of Hispaniola, now divided between Haiti and the Dominican Republic, to Ferdinand and Isabella four centuries ago.

> Its lands are high, there are in it many sierras and very lofty mountains. . . . All are most beautiful, of a thousand shapes; all are accessible and filled with trees of a thousand kinds and tall, so that they seem to touch the sky. I am told that they never lose their foliage, and this I can believe, for I saw them as green and lovely as they are in Spain in May, and some bearing fruit, and some at another stage, according to their nature.

The photograph on the following page was taken close to the place to which Columbus was referring. I am told that 90 percent of the forest has been cut down. Most of the deforestation has occurred since 1950. Without the trees, the topsoil is being washed out to sea by the monsoon rains. The wood is used to make charcoal to cook with, but it is harder and harder to grow food because of the soil erosion. People looking at the photograph might say that those Haitians must be really stupid to do this—surely they must see the consequences of what they are doing. Well, when you talk to the Haitians, they know very clearly what they are doing and the consequences, but they have no choice. They are hungry now, and they see the trees, and there is simply no other cooking fuel available to them. They've got into a vicious circle. The next picture shows a steel factory. We know that the gases created by the generation of electricity used in the factory and in our homes is contributing to the greenhouse effect and acid rain. These are going to have very serious consequences for all of us on the planet. We can still choose less polluting (though more expensive) alternatives, but there is reluctance, even in the face of clear evidence that we are not living in a sustainable way, to give up these destructive technologies. Can we begin to explore how thought might change to bring about a more orderly and constructive approach?

Deforestation in Haiti; the wood is used for cooking fuel.

Steel factory, Holland.

DB: The problem you have outlined is a very serious one. Just to amplify it, I saw a program on television about the Amazon forest, where a Brazilian peasant was cutting down trees very rapidly with a chain saw. They went up to him and asked, "Do you know what you are doing?" And he said, "Yes, I do, and it makes me very sad. I just came from another state where they'd made a desert, and I wish I knew a way to stop. But I've got to support my family." At least we can see what is driving him — and we could say that it is unreasonable to expect him to stop supporting his family. But we may also say in a fragmentary way, "He's a Brazilian and who cares about him? We've got to support our own family, and he has to support his." We are pretending that all families are independent, as if nothing is going to happen if everybody just cuts down all these forests. And as for our children, we are going to supply money and education for them, so that they'll make their way in life. But if we go on with what we are doing, they'll have no world in which to do that.

Very few people want to pursue it that far. Indeed, the mind tends to avoid thoughts that might be unpleasant. You can see this with the factory — we might have to pay more for its products, and some people might make less profit. These are some of the consequences that we think are unpleasant, disturbing. The thought of something disturbing actually disturbs the body and the emotions. And the body wants to feel better, so it demands we avoid the disturbance of the mind. In this way a tendency arises to avoid thoughts that might be disturbing, to deny them, to affirm some other thoughts instead that allow us to believe that everything will be all right.

In the same television program they talked to some landowners who said, "No, that's nonsense; they've hardly touched the Amazon yet; it's immense." They might think that the money they hope to make from cutting down the trees and using the land is going to be interrupted, and that they'll become poor like these peasants. Evidently, this would be a terrible thought to think. So they say there's plenty of forest left — it gives them a much better feeling. That's one of the features of thought: it can get caught up in the connection between thought and feeling. Thus you can see that for a long time almost all the people who have been producing acid rain have been claiming that its effects are unimportant, while many responsible scientists claim that they are *very* important. That's no coincidence, because it's much more comforting and it feels much better for those producing acid rain to think that it is unimportant, that they are not going to have to interrupt their money-making activities. Similarly, governments prefer to think that their citizens are not going to have to pay more for power and for other things.

This is one of the features of thought, self-deception. You can see that thought is capable of getting caught in a loop in which it deceives itself in order to produce a better picture, a better feeling. This can be done collectively, even more than by the individual. People can deceive themselves collectively very easily, because of the common belief that whatever everybody agrees on must be true.

ME: I think that a change is coming, because people are starting to be disturbed by images of rising sea levels and destruction of the land, and perhaps this concern can lead us to look at the question of self-deception, which is pervasive and extremely difficult to understand. We all believe that it is somebody else's part of the boat that is sinking, and that it will not affect us.

DB: This is an example of self-deception, which is something that we must discuss. I think that we'll be able to discuss it better when we've gone into the relation between emotion and intellect, perhaps later on. At this point, we can say that whenever something happens that causes people to question their thought seriously, for that moment they are beginning to awaken perception. They're not just running the disks automatically. Up till now the disks ran automatically, producing the answers that would make people feel better.

Coming back to this matter of questions, a window of opportunity has opened up, and if we don't take advantage of it, it will close — these questions don't stay open indefinitely. Gradually the disks adapt to close the window. There is a constant tendency in thought to prevent questioning, to prevent this sort of thing from being opened up for inspection, because it might be disturbing. So the longer we wait, the greater chance there is for this self-deception process to work, unless we fairly quickly do something that is really to the point.

We have to begin with calling attention to the deeper source of the problem. While this window of opportunity is open, we have to take advantage of it to get people looking.

ME: I have tried to show through the juxtaposition of some of the photographs in this chapter that our problems are common problems. As you

Dust storm, Wollo province,
Ethiopia, 1984.

Dust storm, Cimarron
County, Oklahoma, 1936.

say, it is vitally important that we see the root cause, because our whole approach has thus far been to look at particular examples of the environmental problem in a fragmentary way.

DB: I think your pictures clearly reveal that we are trapped in fragmentary thought about our problems. Indeed, they show that people just solving their own special problems have created the dust bowls, along with all the other environmental problems. Every farmer is just trying to make a bit more money for his family—whether he be the American farmer of the 1930s or the present-day African peasant farmer. Each one feels pushed by these things. Neither looks at the broader issue; each is just pushed. It's only when we begin to perceive the broader issue that we see that we are all pushing each other. Where indeed does all the pushing come from? It comes from other people, and these other people are being pushed by us in turn. If we began to think differently, maybe we could all get together to stop this.

We have got to question this fragmentary kind of thought. Evidently the farmers in the pictures cannot deal with this. How can these African peasants deal with it? You may say that we don't care all that much; they're somebody else, just African peasants. We'll ship them a little help, collect some money for them. But something much more fundamental is needed, which is to say that it's our problem as well as theirs, and we have to have a dialogue. When we talk together, we have to do so as equals, because we are all in the same boat. Our technology may give us an illusion of superiority, we may not notice it at the moment, but it is becoming more and more evident. If our present activities continue, it could easily happen that the entire grain belt of the Northern Hemisphere could become a desert, and in that case America would become very poor, the same as Africa. The whole world would starve. A billion people might die.

ME: One of the problems is that we don't really *feel* we are in the same boat. We pay lip service to the idea sometimes—we imagine that there are no countries and that the world is one—but this does not go very deep into the consciousness from which our actions ultimately arise.

DB: The isolation comes from the way we think. We are drawing false boundaries between ourselves and other people, and we experience these boundaries in our feelings. Unless our thinking changes, any change of feeling can't really be sustained, and so, as you have said, the overall change will not be very significant.

ME: There are every now and again occasions when people feel this sense of emotionally belonging, being part of one world. There have been these concerts to raise money for aid to the Third World, for example. For a certain period I think many people did feel that such activities took people beyond the limits of their own personal lives. But as you pointed out, this sort of thing will not last very long; we need to pay serious and sustained attention to all this. Lots of things stand in the way of our doing that, things that seem more important, or more immediate anyway. It's very difficult in the world as thought has constructed it actually to pay proper attention to these fundamental issues. A lot of people may read this and feel that it is important, that there is a sense of truth in what is being said. But it is very easy for it to get swept away in everyday life.

DB: Everyday life is pervaded with another kind of thought. Such thought is what generally decides what is important and what is not. For example, this everyday thought decides that it is important for you to make your living, to have a family, to get ahead in your company, to protect your country, to back up your religion, to make money, to develop more roads. All this contains implicit values that drive you. That is to say, the collective thought of humanity contains values that are contrary to what we are saying here. It's not primarily the politicians who are doing it, nor the businesspeople. It's not because people have bad motives, but rather it is because of the ordinary, everyday person pursuing his or her ordinary, everyday life, who is caught up in this web of thought. Being caught up that way, people quickly get overwhelmed and forget what they were thinking about. So we need a sustained attention to thought.

Even if we were to take some concrete practical steps to reforest Africa and to do all sorts of other things — stop the emissions that produce acid rain, reduce the production of carbon dioxide, which is changing the global climate, and so on — still, vast numbers of poor people are going to be driven to do all sorts of things against the ecological balance unless we all feel responsible for them. And the basic pattern of our thought is that we do not feel this way. The ordinary, everyday person has an everyday family life and an everyday working life and does not think that way. Most of what you can generally think and read has it the other way. We have to notice this, and we have to bring things up and ask, for example, Do you really not care that your grandchildren and those who follow them are going to starve to death and fight for the little that may be left, as long as you can have your hamburgers today? Most people will agree, of course, that this can't be right. But the disk keeps pushing away that question, saying or implying that it's not an important question. The disk generally determines what questions seem to be the most important.

ME: So thought is really orchestrating pleasure, diverting attention from these serious issues.

DB: And pain. And fear. It orchestrates the emotions of pleasure, pain, fear, desire. It's as if we let our disks compose our music for us. I don't think people are ever going to make very good music that way. In any case, our own disks are far less intelligent than the computer disks.

ME: It's difficult to grasp all this, because it is so pervasive that it seems to be invisible (as the water might seem to a fish).

DB: This is in part because most people lack the ability to grasp abstractions; that is one of the problems. Abstractions are actually very significant. In fact, abstractions have produced science and technology with all these problems. The fact that health has improved and the birth rate has gone up, the nuclear problems, the carbon dioxide — it's all due to abstractions. But people don't take them very seriously. Our education has not developed in us the ability to grasp the importance of abstractions. It is, on the whole, a very poor education anyway, and this is indeed part of the overall problem. I think we'll have to begin with those who *can* grasp abstractions, and we'll then have to try to bring these abstractions to wide public notice in a way that people can understand. And that requires creative action. That becomes part of the task, which is not only to understand these abstractions but to understand how to make them alive in the present to people generally.

ME: Can you explain this more fully?

DB: To abstract means literally to take something away, to separate something from its context. It's very similar to the word *extract*.

The question is, Why should you want to take something away from its context? This is what thought is always doing. It picks on something that seems to be relevant and important and tries to discuss this in the abstract, because that simplifies it and enables us to focus on the main point. The opposite of the abstract is the concrete. The word *concrete* comes from the Latin word *concrescent*, meaning "grown together." You may imagine a jungle with a vast amount of concrete reality. You are generally, however, interested not in the whole jungle, but rather in certain animals or certain plants. In your mind you abstract a plant out of that vast jungle and say, "My mind is on that plant, I want to find that plant, because I want to eat it." You can see here the importance of abstraction. Even animals must abstract what is relevant in this jungle.

Reality is everything concrete and is much too much to be grasped by the mind in detail, so you make abstractions — call that foreground — and leave the rest as background, which you don't notice very much. In this process of abstraction, the word calls attention to something and gives it shape. For example, we have a very patterned carpet here in this room. Once I lost a coin on this carpet and couldn't see it. But I saw a glint, and as soon as I saw this I saw the coin. The glint enabled me to abstract the coin from the carpet; otherwise, it was lost in the details of the pattern.

We are constantly even in such elementary ways using abstraction, and we build on that. Indeed, every name is an abstraction of a class or category like water, air, fire. Even the name of a person is an abstraction — it doesn't tell you all about the person; you usually associate with it a few things about that person.

Knowledge is built up from such abstractions, which are then abstracted yet further. For example, you have chairs, tables, bookcases, and you abstract that as furniture. You can abstract the furniture further as material objects, and you can go on in this way to more and more general abstractions. This hierarchy of abstractions enables you to reason.

By abstracting you do two things: first of all, you leave out the vast complexity that you can't handle, and secondly, you begin to put some order into it, a logically coherent order, which enables you to reason. The word *reason* is based on the Latin *ratio*. This can be a numerical ratio, as with two numbers, like three over four. But a ratio can also be taken qualitatively: as *A* is related to *B*, so *C* is related to *D*. For example, as two things are related in thought, they are related in reality. Using abstract *ratio*, or reason, you can start from some fact and come to a conclusion.

Without abstraction we couldn't function; thought would be of no use; there would be no point to it. The choice of abstractions may be partly by memory, which tells you what is important, but it should also involve direct perception, to see whether the object of our thought really is as we think, or whether our thought is not working coherently. But if you are too stuck to your thought and identified with it, you can't change it by such perception.

So we really need to be able to change our abstractions when it is necessary to do so. But to do this, we have to see that they *are* abstractions. This is often difficult, because abstractions, though insubstantial in themselves, can produce substantial concrete results that, in a cursory inspection, give the appearance of an independently existent reality. For example, we may feel that a country is such a reality. But without the abstract thought of a nation, the country would vanish. If people didn't know that they belonged to a certain nation, there would be no country, in spite of all the houses, factories, legislation, and so on. Nobody would know that it was all related, that it made up a particular country that, for example, must be defended at all costs.

The essential point is, then, that abstractions can produce sustained concrete results, and that thought loses track of this. In a way that we have described earlier, it then calls such concrete results independent realities. It then says, "I'm only telling you about this concrete reality." This leads to confusion. It means, for example, that you might now try to correct this supposedly independent reality while your abstractions are working constantly to prevent you from correcting it. Indeed, they are constantly making you re-create it as it was before, while at the same time you make another abstraction that says you should change it. That may happen in a revolution. We see the terrible mess in society. We take this mess as a concrete reality independent of thought, and we make an abstraction of a revolution to change it. However, we have all sorts of other abstractions in human relationships, such as who's the boss, who has power, and so on. So the revolution produces basically the same sort of society, with just a change in its details.

ME: You are calling for a new kind of intelligence.

DB: Yes. We need a new kind of intelligence because we have created a world that requires it. In the Stone Age the ordinary practical intelligence was good enough. People then had an instinctive sort of intelligence developed somewhat by culture. But today we have created a complex world based on the abstractions of thought. To deal with nature we need a certain kind of intelligence, but to deal with thought we need a much higher sort of intelligence.

We tend to think that thought *is* this sort of intelligence, but it isn't. The key point about thought is that it is like the program, the disk, that responds to the situation. There is no reason why a disk should respond intelligently — a thing might change, and the disk might no longer be appropriate. It responds quickly and automatically according to what has been programmed into it. Similarly, what we have been thinking and learning is programmed into our memory. It's not merely a picture of what happened in the past but a program for potential action. That program is extremely subtle; to deal with it takes much more subtlety than to deal with the objects the program deals with.

Here we come to what I call the process of thought. Thought has a content, that is, a certain substance or meaning. The content may be art or science or history or human relationships. But at the same time it is an actual process going on in the brain and the nervous system. As for memory, we don't know what its source is. Scientists have not solved that as yet. But whatever memory is, we don't have to know about its source. It is enough for our purposes here to know roughly how it operates.

We have this memory, and it acts in a process. A process proceeds; that is, it moves in a somewhat regular way that we can learn. Consider the weather, for example. Originally it was thought to be produced by the decisions of capricious gods. Because the weather appeared to be arbitrary, this explanation seemed plausible. We have now learned that the sun evaporates water from the ocean, that the winds blow it across the land, and that in certain conditions this water vapor cools down, condenses, and falls as rain, ultimately to flow back down to the ocean. A very complex process is going on, involving pressure changes, clouds and wind and rain, and the heat reflected from certain areas. Thus, if you cut down a forest, you may produce more heat, and the water vapor won't condense — it's a very complex process.

In the past, people may have just prayed to the rain god. Now we say that it is a process. We don't understand it fully, but at least we see that it is a process. And insofar as we do understand it, we can predict it to some extent, and adapt to it. We are even beginning to look into the process of maintaining or changing climate, and we can now act more intelligently in this regard if we want to.

So we understand that there is this process of the weather. But as for thought, nobody ever looks at it. We just take it for granted, the way people used to do with the weather. It's as if we supposed that inside us there is a thought god who produces thought, according to arbitrary whim. That thought god could be called "I" or "me" or "the self." Thus is it implied that each of us is somehow in control of his or her own thoughts. But what I am suggesting is that, as a process, thought moves, for the most part, on its own, and that there is little possibility of this process coming to order until we understand it fairly well.

ME: Given that we don't actually see thought as a process, we don't see it as something that can be brought to order.

DB: As I just said, we think that we are controlling thought, but it could be said more accurately that we are generally controlled by the process of thought that we are trying to control. Consider the matter of self-esteem, for example. If I think that I am a great person, I will feel good. But if somebody comes along and says I'm not a great person, I will feel bad. In general, I can't control these reactions. The thought that one is an idiot produces a general disturbance that few, if any, can control. The thought that one is a very competent and successful person may produce a good feeling instead, but this may be false. If so, it may lead one to make serious mistakes out of overconfidence. One can't, in general, control that either.

ME: Let us look back at what you were saying. Suppose that someone says you are an idiot. If you really question that statement by asking yourself if it is true, that might interrupt the movement of thought?

DB: There is in this sort of process a tremendous inertia, a pressure not to question thoughts of this kind. Rather, you come out with another thought automatically. Thus, if someone says that you are an idiot, the disk comes out automatically with, "I'm not an idiot, you're an idiot." This comes out so fast that you don't even know it is happening. If it works, you feel better. Suppose, however, that you look at all this, and you say, "I may feel better for a moment, but it's not worth it, because the whole thing is going wrong." For a moment this process slows down.

This is very important, as it is key for getting more deeply into what is actually going on.

ME: The change in the speed of the process gives one the opportunity to see the process operating. You can't see the spokes of a wheel when it is turning very fast. It's only when you slow it down that you can see the movement.

DB: Yes. It's important for the wheel to slow down. When you actually want to do a job you'll find that the "wheels" of the mind are turning very fast. But now, for the sake of our inquiry, we must have a period when such thought slows down. Either individually or collectively, we must be able to have some sort of space in which thought can slow down and we can all look at it. For this, we need not just thought but an actual perception. It is clear, however, that sense perception is not enough here. We cannot use our ordinary senses to look at thought.

ME: If I understand you correctly, you are saying that the way we abstract from reality isn't working properly in this technological world, though it may have worked better in very early societies and, of course, for animals.

DB: Even in our technological society, simple abstractions may generally work quite well. For example, if I abstract this chair, that may be appropriate, because it has some independence. But in more subtle questions coming from technology and complex social relationships, the process of abstraction may break down and cease to be appropriate. My brain may abstract the fact that there are various organs in its "environment"—heart, kidneys, and so on. If it were to notice that there's an extra kidney, it might think that I could make some more money by making it independent (that is, having it cut out and selling it off). That more or less corresponds to the kind of inappropriate abstraction that people are making about what is called the environment.

The very word *environment* is an abstraction, one that is wrong in this context. It abstracts the environment from the person and the person from the environment. It treats the two as different. But the so-called environment is the very source of being of the person. The human being couldn't exist without oxygen, water, food, and so on. Therefore all this really shouldn't be called an environment. It's the wrong kind of abstraction. It separates things that are one. The point is, in order to

Journalist reporting the 1984
drought in Ethiopia.

make abstractions properly, you have to be perceptive, to see in each case whether or not it is appropriate to abstract in the way that you have done.

We can see the need for such perception when we consider what this picture could mean. Evidently, this picture has to be understood as part of a broader context. This is true of all pictures, but it is especially clear in this one because the photographer in the picture is photographing something that is not in that picture. You're immediately and rather forcibly reminded that this picture is an abstraction and, indeed, one that is basically incomplete. It can only be understood as part of a bigger context, from which the photographer in the picture has chosen to abstract something other than this person who is lying down either dead or pretty nearly dead in front of him. Either he has seen something even more horrific than this, or for some reason something else interests him. You can see that he could have photographed this, but he chose to abstract something else, which perhaps (for all I know) is more significant.

People are, then, trying to remedy the environmental situation in the same way that the photographer is abstracting things to look at. They abstract various parts of what is happening and call each a problem, whatever it may be — whether it is trees or food for these people or something else. But it isn't really the problem. For "the problem" is part of the whole context, just as your picture is only a fragment of a much larger context. Everybody has been looking at these bits of abstraction and trying to solve the abstractions. The only time you can solve an abstraction, however, is when there's really something abstractable, that is, something that is not closely connected to the rest of the context. Science aims at this sort of abstraction. Here, we don't have that, so the ordinary scientific approach won't work in this case. You have to get a perception of the whole. But then you say that the whole is the whole world. It's all of nature, all of society.

However, even that is not enough, because the whole includes thought. Quite a few people see the need for considering a whole — the whole world, the whole society, the whole environment. But then they say or imply that the thought we are using is outside that picture. But this thought is not only in this world, it has created this visible world, and without that thought we wouldn't have this mess. There are certain

Children playing in a tent, Copenhagen, Denmark.

Children watching a solar-powered television set, Niger.

ways of thinking that make the mess we have been discussing here. Thus, in many countries, people's way of thinking leads them to fight wars while they are starving to death. While people fight these wars against each other, they destroy the planet, because their thought says their national and political struggles are more important.

Many people have laid this sort of behavior down to some kind of aggressive instinct. But there is no evidence that without thought such instincts would lead to this kind of meaningless and self-defeating violence. The available evidence about early hunter-gatherer groups indicates that they were fairly peaceful compared with us. They did fight occasionally, but there was nothing like organized war with the ferocity that we have today. It's thought that creates this, by inventing differences that are regarded as so important that you can kill and torture and sacrifice anything to maintain them.

ME: Ours is an age darkened by huge fears: the feeling of optimism that developed after the Second World War has gone. There is a growing understanding that our worldview is leading to greater and greater instability. Inwardly most of us experience a great deal of unhappiness and boredom. One can see no value in all this, unless it leads us to an inquiry that could bring about insight into its source.

DB: It is certainly true that people are generally rather bored. The picture of children in the tent in a housing estate conveys a sense of boredom, with the rigid fixity of life in this estate along with a kind of anger at growing up in such a bleak environment. On the other hand, the nomadic children in the desert watching solar-powered television are bored with the limitations of their way of life and fascinated by the modern world that the first set of children would like to escape by living in a tent. In both cases, the children are unhappy with the uncreative routines in which they have to live.

In my view, this is a problem going quite far back into the past. I think that people who live completely in nature (for example, in the Stone Age) live a life that is not boring, although it might often be difficult for them. However, some people question even that it is generally all that difficult. Thus, if the area was not overpopulated, it took ten to fifteen hours a week to get the food that was needed. They didn't have the luxuries that we've got, but they didn't expect them. The rest of the time people were free, and they could enjoy themselves. Some illnesses they couldn't handle — they had their problems. But you could say that they were much less bored than we are now. With the establishment of civilization, with its regular, fixed pattern of life, one is not nearly as creative. Indeed, for most people in our society life does not offer much that is creative. Usually they work in a factory or do some other sort of job that is rather routine and limited. Children in primitive societies were going around with their parents and taking part in the whole of the activities of the tribe, learning all the time. Now they just sit around unconnected with anything that is going on.

All this is because of our way of thought. You can see that people then thought differently about children than they do now — they thought differently about everything. We have developed a way of thinking that says we must get these products at all costs, no matter how boring the process is. The highest value is to get material products of various kinds, to get money to buy them. It may be boring, but you've got to do it. At this moment most people would not consider the notion that we should produce a more interesting life that would be more frugal. There are some people who are thinking that, but they are only a small minority. They may, however, be the seed of something greater.

ME: Ernst Schumacher once said that one should live as elegantly as possible with as little money as possible.

DB: It is also necessary to make as good a use of natural resources as possible. In addition, people should pay more attention to culture. Our culture is becoming quite impoverished. For example, we produce better and better television systems, but the programs get worse and worse. And people are not interested in the content, but only in the objects themselves and the fact that they make money for the people who produce them and sell them. So the culture is gradually degenerating. The devotion to culture is much less than it once was. Consider, for example, a place like ancient Athens. It had a small number of people, who would be very poor by our standards. Yet you can see what they produced. Our society, with all its wealth and power, is incapable of producing anything like that — it's really mediocre. Later, we must discuss how society developed in that way — it's a long process, involving the way thought and culture went.

ME: I would like to show you a picture of a forest being cut down to enlarge a cattle ranch. This is a picture that I find very disturbing, because it reveals a ruthless disregard in our culture for the value of nature; even though this area of jungle has been killed, it is still disturbingly beautiful. By contrast, a good relationship to nature is beautifully expressed by Krishnamurti, in this quotation from his journal:

> There is a tree by the river and we have been watching it day after day for several weeks when the sun is about to rise. As the sun rises slowly over the horizon, over the trees, this particular tree becomes all of a sudden golden. All the leaves are bright with life and as you watch it as the hours pass by, that tree whose name does not matter — what matters is that beautiful tree — an extraordinary quality seems to spread all over the land, over the river. And as the sun rises a little higher the leaves begin to flutter, to dance. And each hour seems to give to that tree a different quality. Before the sun rises it has a sombre feeling, quiet, far away, full of dignity. And as the day begins, the leaves with the light on them dance and give it that peculiar feeling that one has of great beauty. By midday its shadow has deepened and you can sit there protected from the sun, never feeling lonely with the tree as your companion. As you sit there, there is a relationship of deep abiding security and a freedom that only trees can know.
>
> Towards evening, when the western skies are lit up by the setting sun, the tree gradually becomes sombre, dark, closing in on itself. The sky has become red, yellow, green, but the tree remains quiet, hidden and is resting for the night.
>
> If you establish a relationship with it then you have established a relationship with mankind. You are responsible then for that tree and for the trees of the world. But if you have no relationship with the living things on this earth you may lose whatever relationship you have with humanity, with human beings. We never look deeply into the quality of the tree; we never really touch it, feel its solidity, its rough bark and hear the sound that is part of the tree. Not the sound of wind through the leaves, not the breeze of a morning that flutters the leaves, but its own sound, the sound of the trunk and the silent sound of the roots. You must be extraordinarily sensitive to hear the sound. This sound is not the noise of the world, nor the noise of the

47

Destruction of the Amazon rain forest.

chattering of the mind, not the vulgarity of human quarrels and human warfare but sound as part of the universe. (*Krishnamurti to Himself* [London: Victor Gollancz, 1987], p. 1)

DB: I think that this gives a very good expression of Krishnamurti's attitude to nature, which was a key part of his whole approach. In civilization as a whole, we get so occupied with all the activities of society, most of which are unnecessary, that we hardly notice nature at all. We regard it just as a means to achieve wealth, something to be exploited, or else as a place to go to for a vacation. So-called primitive peoples don't have that attitude at all. Even we in the West didn't have it in the last century. It was then quite common to have a different attitude to nature. But now you can hardly cross any part of eastern America, for example, without running into sprawling and almost merging cities or else the pollution coming from them. You get a feeling that no part of nature is safe from that. As Bill McKibben brings out in *The End of Nature* (New York: Viking, 1990), you could once have thought of nature as vast and essentially free of all that. But now you can see that it is all at the mercy of what human beings are doing.

It creates a different attitude to nature to realize that humanity is able to destroy all this and is very likely to do so unless the present course of development is changed.

ME: As an example of our power to affect nature destructively on a large scale, I am reminded that there was once a plan to use the Grand Canyon as a water reservoir in order to generate electricity. Can you imagine defiling such a place in this way?

DB: And as you have shown earlier, there is another plan for cutting down the Amazon forest for various short-term and even trivial gains. Perhaps all that electricity will operate the television sets showing these impossible programs!

Development, which is called progress, has become a menace. As long as there is money to be made by developing and money available to do it, it seems almost impossible to stop it. You may resist it for a while, but they are going to keep working until they find a way around it. That is, again, the way we think. Development is thought to be absolutely necessary, so that we mustn't stop it, no matter what it does to destroy the ecological balance of nature or its beauty, or to turn our cities into

The Grand Canyon.

unlivable jungles of concrete. But we've got to stop this heedless rush into development, because that way lies a meaningless life and eventually disaster.

There is hardly a politician who would dare say that sooner or later this sort of growth must stop. Yet you can see that such growth must ultimately destroy the world. Thus, as we pointed out earlier, if all the nations in the world tried to obtain the present Western standard of living, our planet would be devastated. Just to consider one point alone, the amount of carbon dioxide would multiply by many times. Indeed, you can apply the sort of calculation that I have made about population growth to the economy instead. If the economy grows by 2.5 percent per year, which is very small, in a thousand years it will have grown ten thousand million times! We will have to stop it somewhere, and it is clear that we have passed the point at which we should begin seriously to consider what would be a right approach to this whole question. For it makes no sense to go on giving growth such a high priority, so that it ultimately overrides almost everything else. What is of primary importance is to have a healthy ecological balance in nature and a good quality of life for everyone. Within the context of these requirements we can then see the kind and degree of growth that is called for.

It is very hard for people to change their thought about all this, however. What prevents us from stopping our present unintelligent sort of growth is ultimately the thought that the continuation of such growth is absolutely necessary and that we can't live without it. But we can live without it, as long as we don't make these material products the main point of life. For example, we have to reorganize life fundamentally so that we don't flood our roads with cars. We have to have other ways of getting around, or perhaps we may not even get around so much. We may instead try to make our living places, our cities, so good that we don't have to rush off to somewhere else. All that would mean reorganizing life almost totally. The general momentum of the last few hundred years is in the wrong direction. People have thought mainly of progress, growth, and development as the prime goals of our society. But this movement has by now become destructive. One could indeed say that Western countries have already carried their current lines of development too far, while the other countries cannot stand much further development of this kind.

It is clear that we have a crisis developing. And if we go on with this momentum, the end is certain; it is only a question of when. Will it be in fifty years? or in a hundred years? It's hard to estimate. But you can see that if we continue to grow for a thousand years, we'll have overgrown ten thousand million times—there will be nothing left on this planet or on any planet around it. You see the power of that thought of growth? It has tremendous power—it is only an abstraction, but it has all that power.

But how is this abstraction to change? People don't see the meaning of abstract thought. They're not used to thinking about abstract thought. As I've said earlier, we have got to develop the ability to see what abstraction is, to see its power. These abstractions are doing the job. The abstractions are actually concrete realities when considered as an actual process. That is to say, the process of thought itself is a concrete reality whose product is abstractions. This concrete process is running away with us. The first thing is to become conscious and aware that this is happening, to find ways to enable people to appreciate the importance of these abstractions. They are not really just shadowy abstractions; they are being projected by a concrete process that produces very big concrete results.

We must talk about how all this came into being, how we got caught up in this mess, and also about how we may look at thought. Perhaps in this book we can make a beginning.

Chapter 2

TECHNOLOGICAL ASCENT AND PSYCHOLOGICAL DESCENT

MARK
EDWARDS:
In this chapter I would like to look more closely at the way technology, and the thinking that has produced it, has changed our lives, not just outwardly but inwardly as well. Perhaps we can begin to find out why there has been so little psychological evolution, despite the invention of so many extraordinary machines that require the exercise of great responsibility if they are not to cause irreparable damage to nature and ultimately ourselves. I think it might be helpful to begin by looking at the technological ascent of society, starting with hunter-gatherers.

I stayed with a small tribe of Campa Indians in the Amazon rain forest. They had very little technology — in fact, they hadn't even invented the wheel; perhaps they had no use for it in that terrain. But the men were very skilled hunters with bows and arrows, and they seemed to be able to find plenty of food close to their homes. They strolled into the jungle and came back with all kinds of very nutritious things. They planted a few vegetables, but they mostly relied on nature for their food and for medicines. They seemed to spend most of their time in the camp, talking to each other — endless conversations and laughter. While they were healthy they had a good life; they seemed very happy. However, they didn't generally live to a very old age, and I was told that many babies died. There was a fairly constant number in the group — about twenty men, women, and children. What I observed was a tremendous sense of pleasure in each other's company and an enormous amount of cooperation. Someone would cook a meal, and everyone would go to his or her hut and eat it together. Later someone else would get food, and they would move to that person's hut. There weren't the divisions between families that we have; children grew up as part of the group, without so much psychological dependence on their own parents. I never heard a child crying. This is quite different from our world. We have gained technology, but we seem to have lost the sense of delight in being alive that I felt the Campa Indians have.

Do you think that the kind of thinking necessary for the advancement of technology destroys something precious in the psyche?

DAVID BOHM: I suggest that what is behind this destruction in the psyche is not just technology, but the development of the whole process of thought. In my view, the tribe you just described must have been thinking significantly differently from the way we generally do. For example, they were not thinking so much that one person owns a particular bit; they were probably not thinking of the separation of themselves from nature and that it was there to be exploited. Some anthropologists, such as Lucien Lévy-Bruhl, have said that they had a more participatory kind of thinking. The word *participate* has two meanings: "to partake of" and "to take part in." They partook of nature and also partook of their food in common. And they took part in common activities to sustain the life of the whole group.

ME: That fits very well with my observations. Their "bank account" was all around them and it was shared. They lived off the "interest." By contrast, as Lloyd Timberlake has pointed out in *Africa in Crisis* (London: Earthscan, 1985), we are overdrawing our environmental bank account and living off the capital. But this tribe I visited wasn't destroying the balance of nature, even around their camp.

DB: They were not threatened by other groups around them?

ME: They were not threatened by other Indians. But a road was to be built through their land. Their way of life is thus threatened by technological man. Of course, it is well known that there are other tribes in other parts of the jungle who *are* in conflict with each other. So it wouldn't be right to romanticize the Stone Age life as a general paradise!

DB: Let's focus on this particular group. In early times, perhaps tribes were far enough apart so that they didn't get in each other's way. The key

54

Hunter-Gatherers

Ashaninka Indian in the Amazon
hunting with bow and arrow.

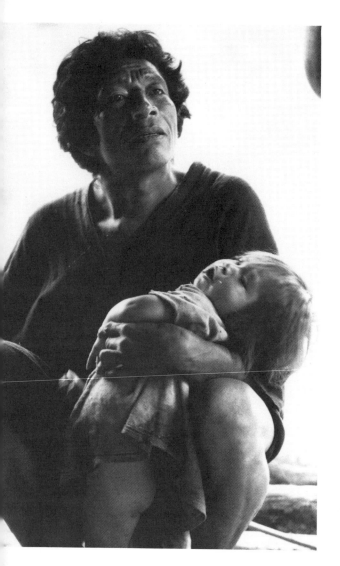

Children in the group are at
ease with all the adults around
them.

Mother with her baby and the
son of a friend.

Baby asleep in a hammock.

Young men in a hut in which they sleep. Several families share one room.

Surui Indians in the Amazon. Two children watch a bulldozer clear a logging road through their reservation. The group needs money to buy drugs to treat tuberculosis and measles caught from contact with outsiders.

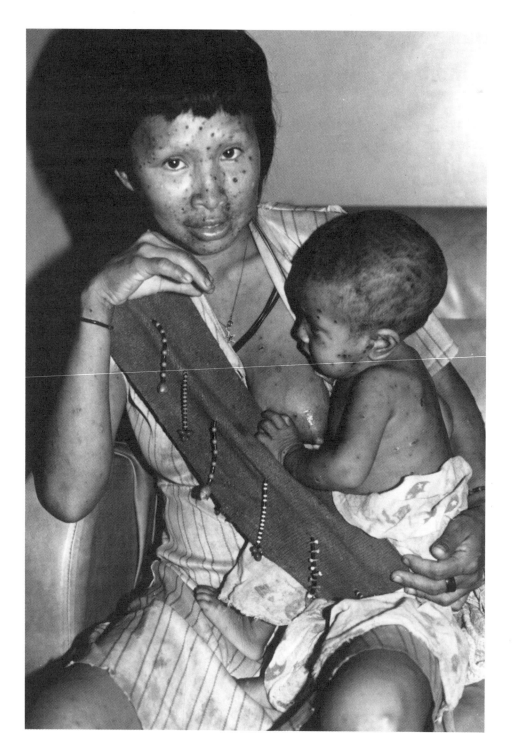

Surui mother and her child wait
in hospital for treatment for
measles and tuberculosis.

point is, however, that their thought was different. But, as has been brought out in your pictures, we now live in a state of widespread and pervasive disharmony and conflict.

ME: I didn't understand their language, but looking at how those people lived, I saw the sheer delight they took in each other's company. You don't see much of that in our world; how often can you see people even smiling in the streets of a typical large city?

DB: You might say that such enjoyment of each other's company is natural to people but that our society knocks it out of them very quickly. It subjects them to such violence and incoherence that it soon goes. Our society has tended to develop in an aggressive, violent, and incoherent way that is exploitative and destructive to nature, whereas in many, or perhaps most, primitive societies it doesn't seem that this is so. There is generally greater coherence and harmony, not only in their emotions but also in their relations and in their thoughts, so that they don't feel so much conflict or social pressure to think one way or another. I had an anthropologist friend named Paul Radin who lived among some of the North American Indians, probably at more or less the same level as the tribe that you describe. He said that there was remarkable freedom among them. You could think anything that you liked as long as you didn't make a nuisance of yourself. If people made a nuisance of themselves, they might be asked to leave the tribe, which was a very bad thing. However, with the greater growth of thought came the requirement that people conform to the thought of the group—be right-thinking people who would agree with everybody else and would presumably support the order of the society in their thoughts. These Stone Age people had a very simple society that didn't need much thought to support it, and therefore they could let their thoughts move more freely if they wanted to.

ME: Some of my friends in Denmark have told me the same thing: that they let their children do anything they like as long as it doesn't hurt another person. And that has become a part of their culture—probably since the 1960s. I think that this has brought about some improvements in their society, but it is not enough to meet the kind of general challenge that we are facing today.

DB: It's much harder to do this sort of thing in our society because, for example, you have got to teach people to think that they must work for a living and fit in in various other ways. We have many more requirements than do these simpler Stone Age cultures. Some people used to think that civilization was making us free, but actually thought was generally getting less free as society got bigger. The more developed a society becomes, the more pressure there is for people to conform in their thinking. There are pockets here and there — Denmark, for example — where people are trying to move in both directions. But you can see that there is an intrinsic pressure in a highly organized society to make sure that everybody conforms, so that they don't rock the boat and disrupt the organization. In a big corporation they would like all the people thinking alike in order to fit in.

ME: For 99 percent of its existence the human race has been made up of hunter-gatherer societies. Our whole psychological and neurophysiological development must have come out of communities similar to the Campa's. But we can't look back at the hunter-gatherers and say we ought to be living like that. Technology has changed forever the very basis of our society. But perhaps we could look at certain developments that have taken place in our thinking, as technology has developed greater and greater sophistication. As we have already suggested, one of these is the way in which the emotions and intellect have apparently become divided by how we think about them and by how we live.

DB: This division has very much to do with the way in which we are related. I think that in the early days there was a relatively simple and creative relationship, in the sense that it was not laid down in a pattern what sort of emotions you had to have or what sort of thoughts you had to have and how you had to fit in. I talked to a woman, Jean Liedloff, who lived for several years with some Stone Age people in South America. (See Jean Liedloff, *The Continuum Concept* [London: Penguin Books, 1986].) She said, in agreement with what you have just pointed out, that over the million years of Stone Age existence we are very likely to have developed certain intrinsic expectations in the body to live in a certain way. Her view is that our present society is violating these and producing tremendous psychological conflict. It seemed to her that life as a whole was generally more creative under such Stone Age conditions. It was not laid down in a pattern or a routine — you could move freely; your relationships were free; there was not this hierarchy, which is a very rigid, noncreative relationship. You must have freedom and free play for creativity, which is very limited in the rigid organization of society, as it is now or as it has been for thousands of years.

To have this sort of freedom and creativity, there has to be a proper relationship of emotion and intellect, in which these are coherent with each other. But at present emotion and intellect are not generally coherent and instead tend to be in conflict. People now often have disruptive emotions, which their thoughts tell them are out of proportion to the actual situation, and compulsive thoughts, which their emotions tell them that they shouldn't have. Being caught up in such incoherence, they are not free to be creative.

ME: This is a very important point. Let us go into it more deeply.

DB: We can all see from experience that emotion and intellect are closely related. For example, a thought about yourself can produce powerful emotional reactions. In turn, we can see that such emotion may clearly affect thought. Thus, when you are angry or otherwise emotionally disturbed, you don't think clearly.

Some light was thrown on this whole question by people who have been studying the brain. In particular, they started by considering an accident that occurred during the nineteenth century in Vermont. (For an account of this, see Richard Restad, *The Brain* [New York: Bantam, 1984].) An iron pin was driven through a man's brain by an explosion and came out, so that he survived. It turned out that it had destroyed a thick bundle of nerves that connect the prefrontal cortex, in which is centered the intellectual function, to the deeper centers of the brain, where you have the emotional functions. This man had been a level-headed person and highly responsible. However, although he did recover, his emotions became totally wild, and he was unable to follow a clear line of thought. The rest of the brain was all right, but this relationship had been fundamentally disturbed. I suggest that we are disturbing it now by the requirements of modern society—not that radically, but still disturbing it in a serious way.

Emotions provide the drive to think. When you get an emotion, you ask, What does it mean? The emotion might be in direct contact with your perception. Thus, if you sense danger, you feel it, and then your thought says, I sense danger; what does it mean? Or your thought might

63

say that this emotion is not in proportion to what is actually happening; thus, you may see that there is no danger. Therefore the emotion goes away: what I saw is not a poisonous snake, but one of a harmless variety, for example.

The emotions and the intellect are thus in a constant direct relationship across this thick bundle of nerves, in some way that we don't fully understand. They are constantly harmonizing, cohering, and reflecting each other. But something may happen to disturb this harmony. What could it be? I say that it is thought.

As I have said earlier, thought is a response of memory. As long as we are concerned mostly with direct perception through the senses or through the mind, the relationship of emotion and intellect works fairly well. The primitive man or woman was certainly very strongly involved in sense perception and must have had some perception through the mind. But people then were not using a lot of highly abstract thought. When we get thoughts that grow and become very powerful in meaning (like the thought of death, for example), this tends to bring about a serious disturbance of the emotions. The memory of what you know about death, when it is stirred up, arouses the feelings. Or one may have a memory of a very traumatic experience, or an experience that was desirable and attractive. For example, you told me that some of these primitive groups were exposed to the products of modern technology and found them so desirable and attractive that they got carried away and wanted to give up their way of life.

ME: As I mentioned, a road was being built through their land, and they began to see trucks and have rides in them and to drink beer and see people with guns. The guns seemed more attractive than their bows and arrows, and they had swapped something of theirs with one of the men working on the road for a gun. Now they need money to buy cartridges, so they grow some extra vegetables, which they sell to traders from a similar background. So they are threatened by their own responses to our technological world.

DB: In early primitive society there were seldom images of things so greatly desirable that people would be that strongly attracted to them. But as technology started to produce such attractive things — for example, golden ornaments — the memory of these could stir up sustained images of such objects to which the emotions would respond very powerfully, more or less as to a perception of the actual thing. In contrast to this, at earlier stages before technology had made this sort of object available, thoughts were generally much simpler, with comparatively few images that strongly aroused the emotions. So with this new development, the system in the brain, which was set up mainly to deal with direct experience, could no longer respond appropriately. Normally, the intellect would send a "message" along the thick bundle of nerves that I mentioned earlier implying that this sort of emotion was not appropriate. But the powerful emotions aroused by such images are based ultimately on memory, and memory doesn't respond in any coherent way to this bundle of nerves. So the ordinary way of thinking that these emotions are inappropriate just doesn't work, because the memory keeps on operating like a disk in a computer.

It is clear, then, that we have emotions based on memory and that we know we have them. We've had a lot of feelings in the past. We can remember them. They come together in a conglomeration that we call an emotion too. This may be a conglomeration of past fears, of past pleasures, of longings, and so on. All sorts of conglomerate feelings based on memory build up, and these "feelings" are really thoughts. For what comes out of the memory is basically a part of thought, even if it includes the arousal of emotions.

ME: Such feelings also affect us physically; the body is highly aroused by anger or fear or pleasure, for example.

DB: Yes. They are also physical — they produce states of muscular tension, rapid heartbeat, surges of adrenaline, and so on. However, there are true emotions that come from direct perceptual experience; they are not dominated by thought but may give information to thought about what is important. Thought has to make abstractions from them. But in addition, thought tries to make abstractions from conglomerate, memory-based emotions that thought itself has produced. However, the thought process now thinks that it hasn't produced them. So the result is very confused.

ME: Yes. I understand — just. When people began to make various objects, some of them giving rise to very attractive images in the memory, the relationship between emotion and intellect began to be disturbed. The trading of such objects must have made them much more available, and this must have greatly amplified this tendency. As civilization developed, this whole process became more and more important. And with the exchange of objects in this way, we see the beginnings of a more complex society with more and more psychological disturbance, which starts to be rather like our own. And as we have seen, the South American Indians are even now being drawn into a similar process, in which they lose their freedom and their natural joy in life.

DB: Some anthropologists have said that there is evidence that even fifty thousand years ago people built up fairly complex societies based on trade but that they couldn't support them, because as the population went up they ran out of food. Therefore societies were built up and collapsed many times. At a certain stage, however, the agricultural revolution occurred, which enabled a large population to be supported indefinitely. We don't know how it started. People knew how to grow plants long before they grew them on a large scale, but at some stage, perhaps because of food shortage, they did it. Then the population increased so much that they could never go back to hunting and gathering. They had to go on, into technology.

It is evident that people wouldn't spontaneously go into agriculture if they could survive by hunting and gathering, because the latter is a much nicer life. But if they are starving, they'll do it. The resulting activity has to be organized because there have to be more and more people doing it. Sooner or later, the group grew too big for people to know each other, so it had to be organized in a fixed way and have people in authority. This development began to break the closeness of human relationships. And so the emotions could no longer be spontaneous. They had instead to be conglomerate, memory-based emotions. Respect for the person in authority had to be guaranteed. To do this, the society had to induce a certain memory of fear in people; otherwise, they wouldn't listen. Then you had rewards and punishment. People didn't want to do all these tiresome jobs, so in order to make people do them, society rewarded them; if they didn't do what was required, they were punished. This system is tremendously destructive psychologically, because the pleasure in the reward and the pain in punishment are registered deeply in memory. One important result is destruction of human relationships. As long as you are looking to other people as sources of reward or are frightened that you may be punished, you are not going to trust them at all: you are going to be careful and hold back.

Desmond Morris, who worked with chimpanzees, gave them paint and canvas and found that they painted all day and didn't want to stop — they weren't interested in food or sex or anything. He thought that there was natural creativity there. Then he thought of rewarding them for what he judged to be good paintings, and what happened was that the quality went down — they did the minimum that would get them the reward. It is a matter of abstracting. If you produce a good painting, you spontaneously get a good feeling, and that is a kind of reward. But this sort of reward is inseparable from the creative act itself. It does not interfere with, and it even encourages, the creative act. We therefore shouldn't even call it a reward, but rather the natural good feeling that comes from doing such an act, which is a sign that it is the right act to do. However, once you can separate the two and abstract whatever produces a conglomerate, memory-based good feeling from the act, it then becomes possible to say that I remember the good feeling and I want to get it again. Therefore, the thing I do is no longer interesting. I am just doing whatever produces the good feeling, and creativity has vanished. Work becomes mainly a routine thing to get through as fast as possible to obtain the reward or to avoid the punishment (which is basically the same thing).

In order to set up society you had, of course, to have routine work, which in itself is not creative. And as I have already said, to get people to do it, you had to have rewards and punishments, which are psychologically extremely destructive. This meant a far-reaching and pervasive change of consciousness for the worse. While technology was going up, consciousness was going down.

Then, when you had accumulated wealth, you had to protect it from the people around. For example, the other hunter-gatherers would "hunt" your cattle and "gather" your crops — they didn't see any reason not to. You had to say that this was immoral and to pretend to have good moral reasons for holding on to your possessions (instead of saying, I just want it, and that's that). Later, to encourage people to fight, they had to be given good moral reasons to do so; thus was created the notion of morality of property, saying that it was immoral to take somebody's property. In a certain sense, it actually was immoral in that new situation.

But the old hunter-gatherers didn't understand that and started to fight. You then had to develop your weapons to fight back, and you then had to say that it was moral to kill and to encourage other people to kill. Then you had to organize the whole thing, and to have armies and authority, and to say that it was immoral not to obey even the most stupid order of a higher officer. You had to distort morality into meaning whatever would support the order of society that had been set up. You can see the whole thing getting generally worse.

As technology developed, people were able to make metal weapons. A few people could then go out and dominate large numbers of people. They then discovered that they could plunder the wealth of others and didn't have to produce it themselves. Moreover, you could make people slaves and force them to produce more than they consume so that you didn't have to work at all.

All this dreary work that technology had brought in could thus be got rid of, while you could at the same time become very wealthy. But then you had to say that slavery was right and instill fear, and engage more and more in self-deception, thus corrupting the mind more and more and driving people further downward psychologically. Slave owners were just as much prisoners of this system as slaves. Slaves lived miserable and meaningless lives, and slave owners lived in fear. They had to deceive themselves about everything in order to go on with it. Even their family relationships were now based on fear. All the openness that you described in the primitive tribe had gone. People no longer laughed as they worked. They worked in pain and misery and fear, and the bosses/owners were afraid that there would be a revolt or that someone else would come along with better weapons and better horses and take it all away — and then they would be slaves. History shows that over thousands of years, this happened time and time again. Some people won, and they were wealthy for a while, and then others came in and took over, and they became slaves. The growth of technology was thus paralleled by psychological degeneration. However, history was often written the other way, saying that people were even more brutal in primitive times. But that picture is distorted. There is no sign that people were worse in primitive times. All the signs are that they weren't as bad. There was nothing like the violence and brutality and self-deception that came later and that have continued in an almost unceasing way into modern times.

ME: This whole development that you have described led eventually to a complex civilization based on a peasant society, which began to spread throughout the world. Indeed, even today a significant part of the world's population still maintains a peasant way of life that would be recognizable to its earliest practitioners. The tools used by peasant farmers in Latin America, Asia, Eastern Europe, and parts of Africa have changed very little. Even the customs and social conditions are similar.

A key characteristic of such societies is that the labor of the peasants supports the political and religious rulers, who are there to protect them against enemies, real and imagined. But those rulers also oppress the peasants and keep them powerless. This is clearly already a very big change in the social structure from how it started with the hunter-gatherers.

Peasant communities tend to be rather conservative, prone to suspicion, and steeped in superstition. This latter has an especially powerful effect on the psyche. Why do you think this tendency to superstition arose?

DB: The kind of thought that will develop relatively complex technology will develop a complex imagination. Through this, it can develop complex superstitions.

ME: It is not generally felt that superstition and technology go hand in hand. The reverse would ordinarily be thought to be the case. Let's look at this more closely.

DB: It was only much later in modern science that there was a movement from technology against superstition. In early days technology was often the servant of superstition. (In ancient Egypt, for example, the priests used their ability to predict the rise of the Nile to convince people of their supernatural powers.) Moreover, technology also provided the instruments of war, enabling the superstitious people to dominate.

In order to develop a technology, you must be capable of a rather abstract kind of thought that thinks of things that are not there and brings them into reality. Images are of things that don't exist. But they may be so strong that they can keep you working until you bring them into existence. That same power of imagination can make images of gods and devils and make them seem to exist too. Thus, in the Middle Ages, hell was considered to be a complete reality. Vast numbers of

69

people lived in terror of hell—we don't have that now to any great extent. You can see abstract thought working. First, people invented gods who would take care of them and a heaven where they could go after they die. They could think about death and how bad that seemed to be, and then think, We won't really die, and if you're good you go to heaven. But then there was the question of what will happen if you're not good. The thought of heaven immediately implied the opposite—hell. The thought would arise that if you're not good you'll go to hell. One could think, The sinners will go to hell; I'm going to heaven. But how do I know I'm that good? God judges. I too may go to hell—therefore I'm frightened. In this way thought by imaginary means tries to achieve security, but it always ends up creating more insecurity and making everything far worse.

ME: To get to heaven, you had to live by a strict moral code, actually put together by thought. Even though what was considered good or bad changed over the ages, it was still not clear that heaven and hell were the product of thought.

DB: And most people were not convinced that they were so good that they were absolutely certain to go to heaven, and many people were convinced that they were bad enough to go to hell. So you can see the rising power of imagination behind science and art and also the rising power behind superstition. It created the power that enabled both to develop.

ME: We are placed in a world in which technology is going to develop. Is it inevitable that the imagination will continue to be used in both a positive and a negative way?

DB: As long as thought doesn't understand what it is doing, this will be inevitable. You are just as likely to produce imaginary creations as real creations. Thus, high technology in Nazi Germany didn't prevent people from being ruled by collective myths that were very violent and destructive and had no more basis than primitive superstitions. Indeed, to a considerable extent, their technology directly served those myths, for example, by providing radios, loudspeakers, and other means of spreading them and intensifying their effects, as well as by providing gas chambers to carry out the mandate of their myths of racial superiority. And one can easily see how similar things are still happening in many parts of the world today, though they are perhaps not, for the

Man with hooks in his flesh, attached by a rope to a trolley that he drags seven miles to a temple. He vowed to perform this penance once a year if he recovered, Karnataka, India.

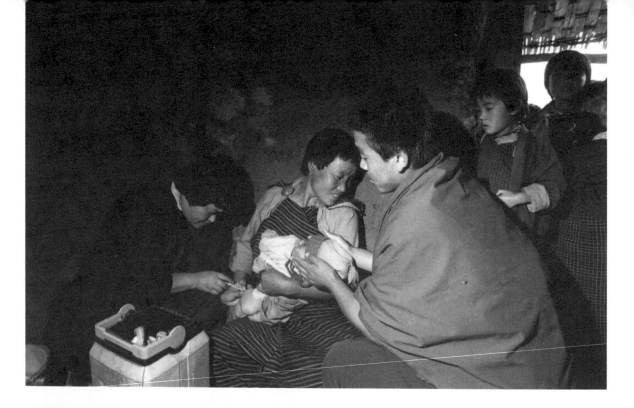

Child being inoculated against measles. The introduction of medical technology to remote places has meant that many more babies survive childhood diseases, Bhutan.

Baby being looked after by her sister, Chhattera village, India.

Mother breast-feeding her four-day-old baby, Kalsaka village, Burkina Faso.

Village market, Fond Parisien
village, Haiti.

Children collecting water.
Kalsaka village, Burkina Faso.

Traveling theater group,
Badalakoppa village, India.

Farmer ploughing his field,
Wollo province, Ethiopia.

Drying wheat in the sun,
Chhattera village, India.

Parsoiya village, India.

Women cleaning rice for the
evening meal, Bangladesh.

Farmer making cord from hemp
fiber, Parsoiya village, India.

A peasant village that has
prospered because of its
proximity to Katmandu, Nepal.

moment, being carried out quite so systematically as the Nazis did their program.

ME: At a personal level, the images one has of one's own past may also cause great sorrow — these too are connected to that same faculty of making very strong images that the brain uses in developing technology.

DB: Thought creates such images, but emotions don't seem to be able clearly to distinguish a powerful image from reality (whether the images are collectively or individually produced). For example, consider the very powerful images that arose when several centuries ago people thought about the dangers of witchcraft. They became as aroused and frightened and angry when they talked about it as they would have while actually looking at witches engaged in the nefarious activities attributed to them. Similar responses (in the form of political "witch-hunts") have occurred in more modern times in connection with other kinds of supposedly dangerous activities. Actually, as has been emerging throughout this dialogue, our whole culture, our whole background, is one in which thought constantly produces such images without knowing that it is doing so.

This is indeed one of the basic things that has been going wrong for a long time. If we could really get to the root of this, I feel that a fundamental change in consciousness could take place, a change that would eliminate the common roots of the basic environmental, social, and cultural crisis that the world is now facing.

In the overall development of civilization that we have been looking at, we have seen that all this tends to get worse as time passes. One important reason is that with the growth of technology, thought is being used ever more extensively and ever more intensively in our trying to shape our whole being to fit the requirements of this technology. In this process, the basic fault of thought, to which we have been calling attention throughout this book, is not even noticed.

ME: Let us now go on to look at how all of this bears on more modern societies, which are characterized by a high level of industrialization and by ever advancing technology. This development, the Industrial Revolution, began in Britain about two hundred years ago. It has continued to develop into our modern, highly sophisticated society, which now dominates the global economy. Nevertheless, in the Third World many people are living and working under conditions similar to those that existed in Europe during the early years of this extraordinary development. For example, these children in the Amazon are making charcoal from mahogany wood, which is used to smelt iron ore mined nearby. What happens to this pig iron? It is exported to Europe, Japan, and America and made into cars and refrigerators. It makes sense to the development experts who advise the bankers to lend money for the smelting furnaces and the mining equipment. It makes sense to the industrialists and the workers who operate the smelters and the children who make the charcoal — they earn a living. It makes sense to the governments in the donor and recipient countries, who see an increase in trade. The Third World governments can repay some of their existing debt, and the Western governments can count on a supply of cheap raw materials to keep their factories operating. And it makes sense to us, because we can buy cheap cars and refrigerators. But when you don't look from these particular points of view it does not make such good sense. Roads all over the world are congested; exhaust emissions from cars are a major source of the so-called greenhouse gases that are changing the climate. A forest that existed for millions of years is being cut down — another cause of climate change, as well as erosion — and children are working at a repetitive job in unhealthy conditions six days a week for a few coins. As you were saying, thought produces these complex processes, and it fails to see the effects.

DB: Yes. For example, the high technology that made possible these metal cans and smokestacks that are shown in the photographs was evidently produced by thought. But without seeing the full implications of what it was doing, the same overall process of thought also produced the rigid social customs, along with the fear and the isolation of people from each other, and the system under which each family takes care only of itself. This process leads each person to say, "I am separate, I have to take care of my family; that's what I need to do, and that is enough." It's all a result of thought; it's all stored up in the memory and on the programs on the disks; and it works automatically. Some person who comes along with more money and sees what is in this picture either doesn't notice it or is a bit afraid and thinks perhaps, "It may happen to me. But no, it won't, because I've got a bank account and a good job." The person gets a nice feeling of security from that thought.

ME: This process of thought is sustained in large part by the way children are educated. For example, I watched how children were taught in a shantytown school. They were told to repeat certain sentences over and over again. You could see them being made to think in a more and more mechanical way. But to survive in a shantytown you really need to be creative. All those shantytowns are not going to go away by themselves; they will only improve if the people who live in them improve them. Pushing facts into the brains of these children as if they were parrots is not preparing them to do that.

DB: These people are continuing to do what they have always done, which is the way thought works — it's on the memory, on the disk. They think that by fragmenting thought and dividing it in this way, they make things more certain and therefore more secure. But it doesn't work. People have been doing this sort of thing for ages, and relationships have constantly been breaking down, and no highly organized society that we know has been stable.

The society that was most stable was indeed that of the Australian aborigines. Some anthropologists think it held for forty thousand years. But it had very little organization as we know it and was rather close to the Stone Age, so it didn't have most of these problems we have been talking about.

People in more complex societies had to try to stabilize them. If you consider the ancient Egyptians, for example, I'm sure that they depended on their priests to help bring this about. The Egyptians went on for several thousand years with ups and downs, and the Chinese in a similar way, and possibly the Indians. The Chinese developed a large bureaucracy and a civil service. Joseph Needham thinks that this is one reason they never developed technology very far. Their bureaucratic thinking tended to hold people in fixed positions; therefore, even though they had a number of ideas that would have been good for technology, they never were able to use them the way people have in the West.

It is clear, then, that no complex society has ever been able to hold for very long compared with the probable million years that we have been human. Roman and Greek society didn't last long even compared to Egyptian and Chinese societies, whereas our present society is actually very shaky indeed and may destroy itself, along with most of the world, in maybe a hundred years or perhaps even sooner.

ME: Yes. Some experts are saying that the natural systems will simply be destroyed beyond repair within two generations if we continue as we are.

DB: It could take hundreds of thousands of years to recover, and whether the human race could survive this, we don't know. If it did, it would be in a very meager way.

To return to the question of the general tendency of societies to decay, one can see that this happens largely as a result of the very measures that were adopted in order to try to stabilize them. Faced with a perception of insecurity, they generally rigidified their thoughts and social institutions, in the vain hope that in this way the tide of change could be resisted. Of course, one of the main legitimate functions of thought has always been to help provide security, guaranteeing shelter and food, for instance. However, this function went wrong when the principal source of insecurity came to be the operation of thought itself. For example, people began to want to be sure that they would be happy, both now and after death. Such thought inevitably induces fear, which results in the disorganization of the whole process. The minute thought projects a future in this way, it must then project the possibility that it won't be so good in this future.

With practical thought, we can take reasonable measures to make it more likely that we will be physically secure in the future. But it is clear that outside this area, no such reasonable measures can really be taken. One may deceive oneself into believing that one can do this (by beliefs about an afterlife and about how the accumulation of wealth will surely make one happy). But one always receives intimations that such beliefs may not be well grounded. This leads one to further feelings of insecurity and therefore to an extension of the whole process along the same lines, until the overall order of the mind starts to fall into a never-ending cycle of disharmony and confusion.

A similar result will follow when society tries to stabilize itself by rigidifying its thoughts, under conditions of change that require precisely the opposite approach.

ME: When do you think this tendency first started to arise? Was it when people began to have possessions that were not just for practical purposes but were required for other reasons, for example, for self-esteem?

DB: Perhaps it began even earlier with thoughts about death, which must have induced a great deal of fear. So even from these early times, there were difficulties that began to disturb people psychologically, evidently as a result of thinking. But at this level of its evolution, society was still fairly coherent and viable.

Clearly, in the search for security, the concept of time plays a key role. Thus, it is known that people as far back as fifty thousand years ago were keeping track of the phases of the moon, probably to help them follow animals they hunted with the change of seasons. That was evidently a kind of move toward greater security. They were at the mercy of the migrations of the animals — if they knew when they migrated, they could do better. Especially after you started to plant, you had to think of the future a great deal. The more you developed civilization, the more you had to organize activities to be synchronized with each other. Time became more important. This was all in the search for order and security, but as I have already said, it went wrong. For thought itself was becoming the major source of insecurity. The thought of my nation, my possessions, my slaves, and so on, could cause tremendous feelings of insecurity, because the slaves might revolt, or some other nation might defeat yours in war and enslave you. Even though you had a big army, you might not be strong enough to resist. Thought aiming for security through nations, possessions, slaves, and so on leads in this way to conditions that actually create greater insecurity. It looked in the short run like security, but thought, being fragmentary, was unable to perceive the long run.

ME: As society becomes more complex, the problems become more complex as well. The intelligence required to uncover all this is greater than it has ever needed to be.

DB: The bigger the society gets, the greater the technology, the more the interdependence. It doesn't necessarily help to have greater communication, because we get an information explosion, people are flooded with information, much of which is misinformation, and that leads to trouble. There is a dream that technology is going to solve all our problems, but this dream is clearly showing itself as false.

Throughout most of the period of development of civilization, religion was the main hope for the people, ultimately including the afterlife and God. It had for a very long time been a factor, but it was gradually built up by thought into something more and more important. Thought, seeing the insecurity in life and seeing widespread misery, began to seek solutions. One of the solutions was for the gods to take care of everything and to protect you. You would just have to sacrifice. And if it didn't work, you would have to sacrifice some more until you sacrificed human beings and so on. And then came a revolt against such religions. People could see that these earth religions had begun to degenerate. Originally, they were probably very good religions (like that of the Hopis, which is an earth religion and worships the earth and the sun and nature). Then as society got bigger, the forces of nature were personified in gods and statues, and the whole thing lost its original meaning. Along with all this, there had developed a patriarchal society, in which war was extremely prevalent, while people were enslaving one another and plundering one another's goods and building up some sort of civilization as they did it. People began to look to religion as a way out of this misery — Christianity developed in that way. And in some ways it helped; it was a movement against the corruption of the Roman society. There is a story by an Egyptian writer called Cavafy about a Roman city that was waiting for the barbarians. They waited and waited, but the barbarians never came. Perhaps they hoped that the barbarians would free them from the intolerable state of their society.

The feudal society of the Dark Ages eventually replaced Roman society and in some ways was an improvement on it, because although it was corrupt, it wasn't as corrupt as Roman society. Moreover, Christianity was a milder religion than some of the others. By the Middle Ages, this society developed a certain amount of prosperity and commerce, and so it created a pressure to move out and get wealth and to move into a new, worldly way, rather than the older otherworldly way. This eventually led to the Renaissance, when the by-now-wealthy merchants began to be inspired by the ancient Greek and Roman culture. They started to move in new directions, exploring, developing science, art, industry.

There was indeed a big surge of creativity at that time. A lot of people began to think that perhaps things would really get better. During this period was laid the foundation of the French and American revolutions. The French Revolution was called by Thomas Paine the Age of Reason, the idea being that instead of the age of faith, in which belief determines everything, now reason would do it. Previously, it was said that faith in

God would bring about order among human beings. But by then, many had given this up. The idea was now that through reason we would establish order among people. You could see in a very short time that it didn't work: people couldn't remain reasonable. Thus, during the French Revolution, they became inflamed with passions and fear and destroyed one another. The same thing happened in the Russian Revolution. It is said that the people who made the Russian Revolution were very aware of what happened in the French Revolution and agreed that they would never let this happen to them. But they couldn't stop it; it happened anyway.

Why should such an irrational response be so powerful in spite of the conscious intention to prevent it? The cause of this behavior is basically the general and pervasive fault of the overall process of thought to which we have been calling attention throughout our dialogue. It is worthwhile repeating this here to show how it works in the present context. What takes place is that thought gives rise to an emotion or an action and then (generally tacitly) attributes this to a reality independent of thought. It then tries incoherently to correct this situation while its automatic reflexive reaction is constantly re-creating it. When this happens, people generally don't see what is going on, and so there are further misinterpretations, which tend to make the problem more complicated still. For example, as you think of another person who seems to be wickedly subverting the revolution, you don't notice that this way of looking is a projection of your previous thoughts onto that person. Rather, it seems that you can see that the other person is actually doing this. As a result, your emotions rise, and your thoughts begin to tangle and twist further, so that you have no control over your reactions. In actual fact, this is all a movement of thought in the sense of the word that we have been using, that is, an automatic reflex of memory, which includes not only ideas and concepts but feelings and neurochemical excitations. As we have suggested earlier, it is a movement of thought as a rainstorm is just a movement of the atmosphere. To attribute what is happening to your own conscious intentions or to those of a wicked person who must be destroyed is like attributing a destructive storm to an evil spirit (that perhaps must be overcome by superior magic).

It is thus clear that this sort of highly incoherent and automatically reactive thought made the revolution and that the same kind of thought ultimately destroyed the revolution. Such thought similarly made

Napoleon try to extend it and stirred up his great ambitions, which led him to be defeated. It is essentially the same as with the tribe that you visited, who saw those wonderful cars that awakened their desires in an irresistible and uncontrollable way. Likewise, Napoleon saw the possibility of conquering Europe and Russia, and it aroused such feelings of desire in his breast that nothing could stop him. He could no longer see clearly. And the same thing happened to Hitler. He didn't want to see the difficulties of conquering Russia. All this illustrates how thought becomes distorted and self-deceptive when we are caught up in the basic fault of the human thought process that we have been talking about.

To go on with the story, when the French Revolution failed, it became the general trend to not expect reason to solve anything. What came instead was the bourgeois society, in which people wanted to take care of themselves, get ahead, and be secure. It was thought that individuals each doing something for themselves would all add up to progress — that was the key idea for that time.

ME: Yes, and as the Industrial Revolution progressed, vast numbers of people migrated from the countryside to the cities, causing terrible suffering among the poorer people. As we said, we can see this happening in Third World cities today.

DB: Yes, and some people were greatly enriched. The idea of democracy was there, but it never quite took hold thoroughly. The trend in that century was not so much toward real democracy and the rule of reason as toward the rule of wealth. The purpose of the whole enterprise was to produce wealth, and eventually it was thought that there would be so much progress made that everybody would be wealthy, and then we would all be happy. I think that was the sort of thought behind it. But eventually it broke down. Most people never got that wealthy, and anyway they squandered vast amounts on wars. The First World War was crazy, all about minor differences. Various reports indicate that at the beginning of this war, a great many people were positively happy that it had come. They thought that it would be over in a few weeks and that they would have a wonderful experience. One may speculate that perhaps they wanted to go back to the Stone Age and its happiness, with everybody sharing. But it turned out that they were stuck in their trenches for four years and died miserably. They squandered immense wealth, and they all became impoverished, whereas they could have

Children learning by rote in a
school in a shantytown, Calcutta.

Children in a slum embracing a
baby, Mexico City.

Children making charcoal,
Amazon.

Despite regular flooding
during the monsoon,
inhabitants of this
shantytown have great
difficulty in obtaining clean
water, Port-au-Prince, Haiti.

Homeless people squatting near
the United Nations Centre for
Human Settlements, Nairobi,
Kenya.

Electrical power plant, Calcutta.

Child drinking water from a
standpipe, Katmandu, Nepal.

Children in a sweatshop making
tins, Dacca, Bangladesh.

Brick factory, Bangladesh.

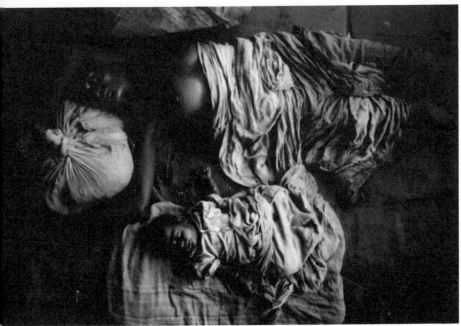

Woman washing pots in an open drain, Delhi.

Shantytown, Lima, Peru.

Mother and child, migrants from the countryside, sleeping on a street, Calcutta.

Overleaf
Behind the Taj Mahal a dead man is being eaten by dogs and vultures, Agra, India. His family and friends were too poor to buy wood for a traditional funeral pyre.

shared it among them, and all could have been wealthy. But instead they just destroyed it all. And they opened the way to the Russian Revolution, which was the last thing that they wanted. When the Russian Revolution came, the communists said, "Now we're going to make everything right." But they couldn't do it. They tried to be reasonable, they tried to be scientific. Nevertheless, they turned on one another and ended up with a real tyranny under Stalin. This was very destructive and prevented the proper development of Russia.

We can see that there has been a widespread wish to do things right. But people assumed that they could do it by thought aimed at solving what they supposed was the problem. People said, Let us look at this problem. It's out there, so let us think about it; let us make a plan, and then we can do something about it. It seemed very reasonable. They all tried, but they all failed. You could either say that they didn't do it right or that there is something wrong with this whole idea, because the problem is not "out there" but "in here" in our overall thought process, which has the pervasive fault about which we have been talking all along.

ME: The tendency is to say they picked the wrong idea or that the solution was too wishy-washy or that there was something wrong in the concept that they were operating with, not in the overall process of thought itself.

DB: Of course, we are saying here that what is wrong is in the general process of thought itself. Indeed, we cannot point to any highly organized society that has been able to sustain a coherent way of thinking, though all have, at one point or another, claimed to do this, or have at least hoped to be able to do this. To add to our examples, we may note that in the American Revolution the people were beginning to produce a relatively stable democratic order, but it eventually broke down, and the states fought a civil war. The intended democratic process that had been set up after the revolution thus failed to sustain public order. Much later, with Franklin D. Roosevelt, people tried to make a liberal democratic movement, and this continued to develop for a while, but it eventually petered out. And now in America the word *liberal* is almost a dirty word, whereas at one time liberalism was the major moving force in its politics. Evidently the liberal notion must be regarded as having failed. The communist idea has also clearly failed. Can anyone point to an idea that has ever really worked in this regard?

ME: If we cast a look back at the Stone Age, it now looks very attractive, at least in certain ways. But we wouldn't want to live in the Stone Age. And in any case, we couldn't; only a few people could survive.

DB: Without our technology, maybe one-tenth of 1 percent of the population might survive!

ME: Our challenge is to live in a technological world creatively. Our challenge is to take this damaged world in which we live with our incoherent way of thinking and come to some kind of harmony both with nature and with technology.

DB: What do we mean by "this world"? Do we mean the world of nature, our planet, or do we mean the world of society? But, as has been explained earlier, the world of society has been created by thought. I would say that there is no way to come into harmony with that world, because such thought is confused, chaotic, incoherent. If you start from this kind of thought, you must continue with disharmony. You cannot be in a harmonious relationship with disharmony. If you want to be in such a relationship, you must have a disharmonious relationship with disharmony.

This presents us with the challenge of how to proceed. The direct action that we might think of taking is not appropriate. We've got to stop and pause and say that here is a big question. For the moment, we should not only stop action, but as has been suggested earlier, we should slow our thinking down a bit. Because if we keep on thinking fast in our customary way, the old disks will give us the old answer that continues the disharmony.

ME: You've been talking about a pattern of decline psychologically in civilization, and at the same time there has been this ever increasing and more and more sophisticated technology that has given certain rewards. People would, however, point out that many of the social problems that existed in the past—for example, the evil of slavery, which you talked about earlier—have been eliminated by social reform. A very large number of people feel that there can be progressive improvement once a problem has been identified. They believe that it can be tackled and eliminated simply by social reform initiated by a group of people paying attention to a particular area in life that has been defined and delineated. What is your response to this idea?

DB: That sort of approach may work for a time in some limited context. I should therefore moderate my statement and say that the general trend has been a psychological decline, but that there have been ups and downs—it was not uniform, and sometimes things got better, while at other times they got worse. But generally as society got more complex, the problems tended to become more difficult. And even when they were apparently solved, as with slavery, the solution was not so clear. Slavery was abolished mainly because technology had reached the point where it was not economical; it had become more profitable to have hired laborers who had more interest in what they were doing. It was only in this context that the efforts of the reformers to abolish slavery had any real possibility of success. What was thus accomplished was a distinct improvement, but still it was followed by a period of serfdom and later by wage slavery, both of which were pretty bad. Even in Victorian times in Europe people still suffered great misery—they were often worse off than the people on the land where they came from, and they had, if anything, fewer rights. Of course, they were better off than slaves, and there was a slow improvement in the standard of living of most working people.

Even so, in many places we find that poverty is coming back. Thus, you have shown pictures of people sleeping on the streets both in London and in Calcutta. So improvement is not a uniform thing. These achievements are evidently not permanent. Improvements are made, and then other forces come up that have been neglected and turn them back. For example, as I have already said, the whole liberal reform movement seems at present to have almost collapsed. Indeed, many people now think that it is soft to be liberal, that people who are homeless are losers, whereas formerly there would have been a much more widespread sympathy for them than there is now. In other words, there has been a change in point of view, a reaction possibly to a period when social programs became wasteful. So the thing moves back and forth, and it is not a uniform progress.

In addition, new difficulties arise. In place of slavery we may have other problems now. People may, for example, feel that life has lost its meaning. It is also not even clear that slavery has been abolished. Thus there are new statistics that say that in many parts of the world there are still many millions of slaves. Indeed, there are children working in the Far East—millions of them—under conditions of slavery that are as bad as they ever were. And this slavery is maintained by the fact that "free" people in technologically advanced nations buy the products of their labor. So it is not clear that there is any steady improvement. This is in the nature of thought: that in its fragmentary action, all sorts of other things are left out, and these go on to make things worse some- where else.

ME: Most people can't conceive of a nonfragmentary way of improving society, one that could be brought about, as you have suggested, by a different way of thinking.

DB: Let's look further at the idea of the fragmentary approach. This was certainly behind the common notion of progress during the nineteenth century. When I grew up in the early twentieth century, we all accepted it. We were saying that not only through democracy and through social change, but also through science, industry, and technology, there would be steady progress. People would get better and better. At that time we thought that the worst problem was poverty, and that in eliminating poverty, the natural goodness in people would take over. But since that time it has become clear that this is not so. In the last fifty years, in certain parts of the world at least, there was a tremendous increase of wealth and yet conditions did not generally improve. For example, there are all sorts of tensions between various groups. Then the drug problem arose because people became bored, or perhaps for other reasons. In America you now have a hundred billion dollars a year in the so-called drug industry. Once you have that much money behind it, nothing can stop its power to corrupt. Moreover, conditions for most people in the Third World have got worse over the past twenty years or so. Also we now have the ecological problem. Almost no one foresaw that. The very movement toward economic growth and the creation of wealth that we have been talking about brought about this ecological problem, which could eventually have worse consequences than the difficulties that it solved; it might mean the end of the human race. In the nature of the case, this fragmentary approach can't really work, because even if it succeeds in its stated objective (which it seldom does), it sets in train other things that it does not consider. And these very often have pro- duced additional problems that are generally even more complex and difficult to deal with.

Modern Society

Children waiting for the school
bus, Seoul, South Korea.

Children watch television while
their parents practice traditional
Indian dance, London.

Kultorv Square, Sunday
afternoon, Copenhagen,
Denmark.

Overleaf left
Frightened children looking out
the door of their temporary
home, London.

Overleaf right
A young man lying in a
cardboard box begging for
money, New York. The sign
says he is too weak to work
because he is dying of AIDS.

The Stock Exchange,
Copenhagen, Denmark.

Street scene, Seoul, South
Korea.

Las Vegas, Nevada.

Sunday afternoon, Southend-on-Sea, England.

Woman playing bowls, Hyde Park, London.

Couple at a rock concert,
Copenhagen, Denmark.

Homeless young man sleeping
under a tree, Hyde Park,
London.

Christiania Can-Can girls
waiting to perform,
Copenhagen, Denmark.

Dance competition,
Copenhagen, Denmark.

The Tivoli Pantomime,
Copenhagen, Denmark.

Amalienborg Palace,
Copenhagen, Denmark.

ME: Perhaps I could bring in the case of Denmark, where I have spent some time. I am very interested in seeing how society there works. They have an economy that seems to have generated a great deal of wealth (although they are also experiencing problems now); tax is very high, and they provide enormous welfare assistance. Successive governments since the war have felt that if you spent money on social problems, you could get rid of them. That simply hasn't been the case. Perhaps because the "cradle to the grave" welfare system takes care of material needs, the deeper psychological problems are allowed to flower. Many people say they are bored. There is a high rate of suicide and almost the highest consumption of drugs in the world.

DB: There has to be. Because of the modern development that puts people into separate compartments, they no longer have their earlier solidarity with their neighbors. They feel isolated. Their jobs are more isolating, so they no longer have a sense of close relationship with their fellow workers. The more we automate industry, the more we isolate people, and the more routine, on the whole, people's work becomes, producing less satisfaction for people in their work and less meaning in their lives. In the 1960s, when we had relative affluence, you found people expressing their dissatisfaction with this state of affairs. Hippies and vast numbers of other people went around saying that such a life has no meaning — and it didn't. When times got hard and they had to hold jobs, they forgot about all this. If times were to be as good again, there would be a vast amount of that kind of dissatisfaction being expressed.

But there are even deeper problems. If we go back to the Stone Age tribe that we discussed, we see that we don't have the free, happy, creative relationship with nature and with other people that they have. What I mean by creative is not merely the ability to produce art and science, but actually to be creative in ordinary, everyday life, in the sense that it is not routinely cut out for you. Nevertheless people cooperate and participate and have a sense of relationship, which they also want in order to feel free and creative.

ME: Anybody who reads this will ask if it is possible to generate that kind of creativity in a society that has developed in such a destructive way.

DB: It is true that conditions in our society are in general not favorable to creativity; they are on the whole very unfavorable. There are a few people who may have opportunities for creativity in art, science, or certain other fields. But even in art, one wonders sometimes. Art seems to have reached a crisis; people don't seem to know what they are doing. In their attempt to be creative, they don't seem to have the clear sense of doing something worthwhile that they had, say, right after the Renaissance, when it was evident to artists quite generally that they were doing something meaningful. Now they do all sorts of things, and the general public doesn't really understand. Indeed, very few of the other artists do, and they are becoming isolated from one another. Science has become bureaucratized and organized on a vast scale so that very few scientists can be creative. I don't see that, in a human way, society is satisfying people's genuine needs along these lines.

ME: Is it actually possible for this sense of meaninglessness that pervades the life of so many people to change through a serious inquiry?

DB: This is our challenge. Our whole approach has to change, or the human race is not viable. Is it really viable under these conditions that it has itself created? It was viable under Stone Age conditions. We have seen that it gradually got less so as technology and civilization developed, until by now its very existence is threatened by nuclear war, ecological disaster, and possibly other catastrophes that our technology may produce in the future. The human race thus far has not demonstrated that it is capable of sustaining life at a high level of technology. This is a question that is open. The exploration that we are making now is the beginning of what has to be done about it. We first have to ask, Why is it not viable? Is it something intrinsically wrong with the human structure? Or could it be the result of something mistaken or something changeable, something that is not intrinsic and that could be different?

ME: Yes. One could even ask whether it is a structural problem in the makeup of the brain itself. For example, if we had one leg shorter than the other, we would limp and wouldn't be able to walk straight. Is there a suggestion in your mind that maybe the brain somehow has evolved in such a way that it is not viable, because it cannot avoid deceiving itself in order to feel better?

DB: I have already made a suggestion earlier about what is preventing viability. This is that there is a normal communication between the intellect and the emotions that is quite all right when there isn't a lot of thought, especially about the self and its sense of psychological security. When there is a lot of such thought, which is, of course, based on memory, the system can no longer correct what's gone wrong. For whatever disturbance is happening is coming from memory, and it doesn't know how to reach that memory. It can only try to reach the results of memory. It's only dealing with the symptoms rather than the cause.

This may not be the whole story, but it is a key part of it. Indeed, I think that there is more to it than this. But I would like to focus on this for a while.

The human race probably evolved with comparatively little of the disturbing kind of thought, and the direct communication across the thick bundle of nerves that I have mentioned earlier was such that emotions and intellect were able to keep in harmony with each other. The system functioned in a generally coherent way. It could go off a bit, but it could be corrected. So, though it wasn't perfect, it was certainly tolerable, if not more than tolerable. With the growth of civilization, however, it was necessary, as I have already suggested, to set up thoughts that were powerful enough emotionally to get people to do all these boring and unpleasant jobs, as well as to stick together, to obey orders, to accept subordinate positions, to do all the tiresome things and take all the unpleasant risks, often mainly for the sake of their rulers and their masters.

ME: It seems to me, from what you have said, that this sort of difficulty arises when thought tries to manipulate itself into what is regarded as a right pattern of behavior.

DB: Yes. You can see this with children. People say to them that if you don't behave, the boogeyman will come. The idea is that you create feelings of fear in the memory of the child to serve as a reminder that a child who misbehaves might have to face the boogeyman.

ME: I was told that if I didn't pass certain exams I'd have to be a postman!

DB: People think that they are helping in that way, but they are actually subtly corroding the child's mind. For they are setting reward and punishment as the general basis of the child's activity. As I said earlier, under such a system, a reward does not come from the creative activity itself but separately from this activity. Action brought about in this way is generally not creative. Indeed, the prospect of a reward gets in the way of creativity, not only because, as I have already pointed out, it focuses our intentions on the anticipated satisfaction of the reward rather than on the creative act itself, but also because a reward is necessarily for some definable achievement. At best, this leaves open only the possibility of the creative development of a means to reach this predetermined end. But full creativity requires that in principle the end itself be constantly open to creative determination.

Thoughts that are arbitrarily limited by offers of reward and threats of punishment can often give rise to powerful emotional disturbances, in which there is a tremendous pressure on the brain to follow rigid lines of activity and to adjust its thoughts according to what society wants. It will therefore accept false and self-deceptive thoughts, saying, for example, that you have to believe in the god the community believes in, you have to accept the basic aims of the society or else you are bad: no one will like you, you won't get along.

Evidently, there are all sorts of other ways of controlling people, including physical violence and various other forms of coercion. What I have given are just some examples of how thought is commonly controlled.

As all this goes on, the whole system is disrupted, and it all goes into the memory. As children grow up, they may seem to forget about this disruption, but it is still on the "disks." When similar difficulties arise that remind them of their earlier experiences, they may feel disturbed without knowing why. The intellect responds with its normal function and says, Let's find out the cause of this feeling, and see if it fits, and from this perhaps I will know what to do. But it can't find the cause. The cause is hidden in memory, which is, in itself, never conscious. So the child can only try to deal with the symptom and try to correct it, which means making it worse. What is then happening, in effect, is that the child is trying to find those thoughts that will stir up better feelings. And vice versa, the emotions presented with the images produced by the intellect don't know that they are images, so they create desires for and against them that are irrational and lead the person astray. The simple and direct relationship between emotion and intellect that would be a proper one has been disturbed. The path now goes through the memory. And who knows what that is? Certainly the intellect and the emotions don't know what memory is. All that they have been able to do is flounder around and try to find something that will relieve the tension.

We all have this sort of stress and tension, which is constantly increasing in modern life. For example, I read somewhere about the case of an air traffic controller. He was under enormous stress. First of all, there are too many airplanes and too few controllers because his employers want to save money. The airplanes are ultimately the result of thought, as is money and the desire to save it. And then, he doesn't get along with his boss. The whole relationship between boss and worker is evidently a result of thought. At home he has problems because of shortage of money (likewise, ultimately a manifestation of thought). He keeps on thinking about all of these; he is stirring it up all the time. In the jungle, faced with the problem of his boss, for example, he would either fight the boss or run away or freeze — but here none of these responses would do any good. So he has to keep on working and going home to his problems. His memory keeps on operating, reminding him of all his problems, stirring up the chemistry and the emotions and the confused thoughts. The whole system is now trying to get it straight, but all it can do is to try to correct the symptoms that appear within the intellect and the emotions. The cause is in the memory, but as I have already said, the system doesn't know where the memory is or how to get at it. Drinking some whisky obscures the memory for a moment, but he still needs his memory. He could drink himself into a stupor, but that would just make another problem, for the next day he has to go to work and be clearheaded. So you have what is called stress, which causes physical degeneration as well as mental degeneration. And relationships break down.

It is obvious that in the hunter-gatherer society as you described it there was very little such stress. It is evident that the more you organize society, the more of it you are going to get. It's also obvious that science and technology, the way they are now going, will almost certainly increase stress rather than get rid of it. They are going to make society more and more difficult the more they organize it, more and more dangerous. For example, the greater our technology, the quicker we can create deserts. I saw a program showing how the Romans created deserts. North Africa in Roman times was the most fertile part of the world; they cut down all the trees, and thus created a desert. After the Romans fell, the peasants with their goats got rid of whatever the Romans didn't get rid of. The Romans, with their comparatively primitive technology, took several centuries to create a desert, but with our highly developed technology, we can do it very much faster.

So science and technology are unable to help here. If we want to do whatever makes deserts, they cannot stop us. Thus, if we say that maximizing the profits of those who grow and distribute food is a key priority of our technology, even if this results in the destruction of soil and forests, technologists are ultimately compelled to invent ways to do this as effectively as possible. They have no choice, any more than the peasant has about sawing down all those trees in the Amazon jungle. Technologists are slaves as much as peasants; the boss is a slave as much as the worker. They are all slaves of this sort of thought. Thought is like fire: it is a good servant, but a bad master. This fire is just running around the world, out of control.

Is the human brain capable of doing something different? We don't know. Again, there are other aspects of this problem that we want to look into; however, this problem is certainly there, and it alone would be enough to end the human race in the long run.

ME: How does one approach a question like this? It requires a creative response, but ordinarily (as you have pointed out) we have been taught not to respond creatively—that's been largely destroyed in most of us. Confronted by the evidence and the sense of our own eyes, we see this deterioration of society. You have pointed out some of its deeper causes. But I would like to see how you would approach actually doing something about it.

DB: We don't know the answer, but we may adopt the sort of attitude that I would call tactical optimism. That is, we will proceed on the assumption that it is possible, although we don't know exactly how to bring it about. All enterprises that people have ever engaged in have required such an assumption.

ME: So we are making it clear that there is no concrete answer that can be given beforehand; this is an exploration.

DB: Until people are aware of a problem, they are never going to do anything about it. So we have to get to be aware of the problem and see what its nature is. I hope that this book is beginning to bring about such awareness. We don't know whether there is time, but I hope there will be. The deterioration may not go as fast as some people think.

We could say that political action is needed to prevent our civilization from sooner or later facing a catastrophe. In such a catastrophe, there would, of course, be little or no possibility of inquiring into the process of thought, which is ultimately the source of the crisis. In view of what has been said here, however, we can see that the most that political action by itself could do would be to buy time — to slow down the overall degeneration. During this time, we would have the opportunity to work on the thought process. Political action on the environmental crisis and the inquiry into the source, the cause of the crisis, would go hand in hand.

However, if we don't use the time that has been bought to get at this source, this cause, there is little point in even buying it. We could say let's plant trees, let's save the whales, and so on. These are very good objectives, and certainly they should be carried out. But unless we get to the cause of the degeneration, something else that is even more complex and destructive will arise that we don't expect. For example, people used to say that if only we got rid of poverty everything would be all right, but they didn't foresee that this could bring about immensely greater suffering. They didn't anticipate that to increase production indefinitely could give rise to worldwide ecological disaster. Therefore we need a much more clear perception of the nature of the problem instead of just saying that getting rid of poverty, or doing something else of that nature, would solve it.

ME: As an example of what you are saying, people are proposing cutting down carbon dioxide emissions, but there are many other subtle factors at work in all this.

DB: What do we have to do in order to cut down carbon dioxide, aside from elementary things like saving energy? As I've said, eventually we've got to stop growth. With our present levels of population, this means that people have got to give up the idea of an indefinite increase in the standard of living, at least in the West, and to realize that their material expectations cannot all be fulfilled. Even if we developed a technology that would produce energy without carbon dioxide, there would be other problems, like pollution, and we can see that technology would give rise to still other problems. Thus, when I was working on atomic energy, it was thought that this would solve everything, but it turned out to create very serious problems of waste disposal, as well as danger of leakage, of plants blowing up, and so forth.

ME: If you could make cheap electricity by pollution-free means, you could bring power into all the villages in Africa and India. This would be a very sudden and traumatic change to their life-style. The consequences are almost beyond imagination. It would certainly create many new problems.

DB: If they have this cheap electricity, what good is it to them, unless they have a lot of other things, and where would they get them? If they start producing goods at the same rate that we are producing them, then they'll destroy everything in some other way. Let's say that there are somewhere between five hundred million and a billion people in the more developed parts of the world. If *five* billion people wanted to reach the Western standard, you would get at least three or four times the amount of trouble. Even if you leave out carbon dioxide, there are all sorts of other things. There is, for example, the sheer overcrowding, the destruction of agricultural land, the fact that fertilizing won't increase food production indefinitely. You've shown photos of land that has been eroded. I've been reading that this erosion is a very serious problem, that large parts of the world (including the West) will be very badly eroded within not too long from now. If you say that we should have organic farming and so on, that is fine, but then people would have to produce less industrially. People will have to accept this; they will have to change their thoughts about it. But their emotions are demanding these goods. What is the relation between thought and emotion? — we have to go into this more deeply. Will you accept your emotions and say that I've just got to have what I desire? Or will you suppress them? That won't work either. So we've got to achieve a harmonious relationship between thought and emotion, or else the human race is not viable. We have begun to inquire into this question here. But I think we should now defer it to our later meetings. It's quite a large subject.

A DIALOGUE
ON THOUGHT

Chapter 3

ON THE NATURE OF THOUGHT

MARK
EDWARDS:
In the first part of the book we discussed some of the causes of the deterioration that has come with civilization, and we found that a basic cause is a certain wrong functioning of thought. Perhaps in this part of the book we may have dialogue in which we may see what it means to come into contact with the actual process of thought. And through this, thought itself may begin to change.

DAVID
BOHM:
But, as was said in the first part, we don't expect to find a complete solution here. Our emphasis must rather be on exploration and inquiry.

ME:
It may, however, be a beginning that can be followed up on in dialogue among other people who become interested through coming across this book and reading it.

DB:
Yes. I hope that people will be able to pursue these ideas among themselves and even by themselves. Think of it as perhaps a seed from which something more might grow.

In the first part of this book we brought out the notion that the trouble arose largely because of the response of memory. As a key example we considered the relationship of emotions and intellect. The intellect is centered in the neocortex, near the surface of the brain, especially the prefrontal lobes, whereas the emotions are centered in the deeper inner parts, with a thick bundle of nerves that connects intellect and emotions and relates them closely.

Let me sum up what has been said about this. If you have a feeling, a thought then comes up out of the question, What does it mean? For example, it might mean danger, and you take appropriate action; or it might mean that there is no occasion for this emotion, and therefore it dies out. There is a two-way relation that is immediate between these centers. As brought out in chapter 2, this was working fairly well in primitive times, when human beings were primarily living close to nature in groups of twenty to forty and there was no authority. Things were fairly friendly; there was little or no routine work that was so repetitious as to require rewards and punishments in order to get people to do it. As civilization developed, however, more and more thinking was needed, and this required more and more use of memory. But such thinking leaves a kind of residue. This means not merely the remembering of incidents, but also of conclusions, such as saying that people of this kind should be dealt with carefully, people of that kind are friendly, plants of this kind are nutritious, animals of that kind are dangerous. In this way some general conclusions are gradually built up and registered in memory.

These conclusions, somewhat like conditioned reflexes, cause you to react automatically. When you see an animal of a certain kind, you don't stop to think. Immediately the memory reacts to provide the right disposition of body and mind, which may be to fight, to run, to freeze, to be friendly, or something else. This disposition may include a tendency for memory to respond with further thoughts and feelings, along with physical responses and the release of hormones and various neurochemicals that are appropriate to the action. Thus, if you *actually see* what is evidently a dangerous animal, the adrenaline flows; the heart beats faster; the muscles become tense; and so on. But if you see an animal that you have been *told* is dangerous, the overall response will be essentially the same. So your whole system is profoundly affected by this sort of response of memory, and it happens immediately, without your having to think. Every time you think, you add to that kind of memory. Also every time something happens, the incident is recorded, and if there are powerful emotions, they too are remembered. Several similar incidents produce a conglomeration of emotions that can be given a name, such as anger or fear. This can be remembered and can be called up again by the word. More generally, memory allows anything to be called up by the word, by the symbol, and communicated. In this way, a vast new field is opened up that makes possible an immense human development.

ME: This obviously isn't something that animals have to any great extent.

DB: That is so. What is particularly significant in the context of this book is the relationship of thought and feeling. We noted that they are not really separate except for the sake of discussion, because there is a thick bundle of nerves that makes a very fast connection between them. This connection is so strong in its action that it doesn't make much sense to regard them as separate. Moreover, thoughts and feelings can connect fairly directly to the physical state of the body and to the perceptions, as well as to the hormones and the neurochemicals, which may arouse you or inhibit you or make you anxious or make you feel well. The response of memory may therefore have a profound effect on the whole system, an effect that may be either pleasant or painful. It is particularly significant that you can be badly hurt in this sort of way by the response of memory, because, for example, you can remember painful experiences that can activate the pain nerves in a way that is similar to (though not the same as) the original experience of pain. Through this sort of process you then feel hurt, more or less as you did originally, for it feels painful even in remembering it. Then comes the demand to get rid of this pain, which is natural. But because the pain is caused by memory, how are you going to get rid of it?

ME: One of the problems in what you have been outlining is that the process clearly started off giving human beings a tremendous advantage over other species, because we were able to build up knowledge about the environment that could then be passed on to the next generation. So we developed a very complex knowledge about the plants that could be used and how to hunt and so on. This process seems both to work to our advantage and also to produce problems: it is double-edged.

DB: As I've said many times, the problems were not very serious in early days, because we didn't use a lot of abstract thought. Most of the thought was connected with immediate experience, where you can directly see whether it is right or wrong. Once you start thinking about abstract things that can produce these powerful effects, however, it is not so easy. Abstract things can impose very powerful emotional reactions on the brain: the fear of a shadow that may be an assailant, or a violent reaction to something that may impugn the honor of your family or yourself (in the period when dueling was common). All these abstract things began to take on an apparent reality, to seem to be as real as concrete things, as well as very powerful. People therefore began to respond to them as if they were real. Had they been able to see them as just shadowy forms, the shadows being mistaken for something real, they could have got rid of them by looking again and seeing that they were only shadows. But if you say that your honor has been offended, where will you look to see whether it has a reality independent of thought or whether it is only a shadow?

ME: One would tend to look to the emotions. But the emotions seem to inform you that this is very real.

DB: In such a case, you are getting misinformation. The emotions are responding to a powerful memory, and this memory need not be a particular incident but a generalized incident called up by a word. The emotions are responding as if you are seeing an animal or as if you had been slapped in the face. Indeed, the start of a duel was to slap the other person in the face, meaning that you had already been slapped in the face, as it were, by what he did. But that slap was entirely symbolic; it came from the "disk" of the memory. However, it was taken as a reality independent of thought. This is one of the features of thought, that it began to lose track of what is independently real and what is produced by thought, because it couldn't keep track of what is projected from memory and what is direct perception and experience.

ME: Are you saying that thought isn't subtle enough to differentiate between these?

DB: Not only that, but the brain and nervous system as a whole lose whatever possibility of doing so that they may originally have had, once the memory becomes full of powerful feelings and full of thoughts of necessity. This happens because memory becomes mentally confused and physically disorganized. Moreover, we have traditions building up memories of tremendous power. The collective thought of tradition carries much greater weight. And it seems real just because everybody shares it. One of the tests for reality is what everybody sees. If everybody sees it that way, we think that it must be so.

ME: Is that test not valid?

DB: It's often a good test, but it is not always so. For as we indicated in previous chapters, we have collective delusions. Indeed, we have seen many cases of whole nations being caught up in such delusions, so that we hardly need to give any examples here. This means that we can't make a complete rule and say that it's always this way or always that way.

ME: But we do want complete rules.

DB: That is because thought is seeking security. The whole purpose of thought is to give you some kind of security, at least as far as that may be possible. It is programmed to look for more security, and it is not entirely wrong to do that. But then it not only tries to get you security by telling you what plants are poisonous and what plants are good with the help of memory, but it also tells you when you have been insulted, what your national identity is and what the other person's is, when you've been hurt, when you've got to kill, and so on.

ME: It might be useful to say that memories in this latter group are dangerous. For memory builds such an incident into an image that is fixed, when in fact the reality is altering.

DB: Memory is not able to adapt to the changing reality. It does slowly adapt, but it is often too slow and often too rigid, especially when the memory contains powerful emotions and thoughts of absolute necessity.

ME: One of the basic features of reality is that it is always changing; one of the tests of memory is its tendency to hold within this some fixed range of forms, so that its possibility of change is limited.

DB: The actual situation is a bit more complex than this, for one of the basic tests for something real is that its changes are also limited, in the sense that it does not change in an arbitrary way. If something stands up to repeated observations, one is likely to conclude that it has been established as a fact. This is a good test for reality in many cases. But it can go wrong. For memory can keep on repeating, for example, that you have been hurt, and repeating a conglomerate of such feelings, and so you may say that this proves that I am really hurt. Thus, one may say that a tree is not merely an ephemeral phenomenon because it is there every time I look at it or touch it, so that it must be real. Similarly, I might say that the hurt is real, because every time I look, there it is! But the difference is that when I look, I also turn on the "disk" (without noticing that this is happening), and I get it again. So something not there appears to be there. In this way you create illusion.

ME: The difficulty, as I understand it, is that we are using a faculty of the brain that is very useful in certain activities—in our practical lives especially—but there is a lack of subtlety, there is a lack of intelligence, in its informing us just where it is useful and where it is not. It doesn't really know its own limitations.

DB: So we need a quality that we might call subtle intelligence. The notion of subtlety is important in this context. There are two qualities involved here, the subtle and the manifest. The manifest is what can be held in the hand—that is what the word means in Latin—or else it can be held in the eye. Basically what you can touch and what you can hold in your eye is what you take as manifestly real. Subtle is then just the opposite. According to the dictionary, it means rarefied, highly refined, delicate, elusive, and undefinable. In addition, it is interesting to consider the root meaning of the word in Latin, which is *subtex*, signifying finely woven. This suggests that thought could be regarded as a net of a certain degree of fineness. But being based on memory, it cannot be very fine. For it has to fix certain things, and when a more refined perception is needed, thought can't provide it. It only knows certain things, based on what we happen to have picked up in the past and learned and what is registered in memory. Thought based on such memory produces that net and tries to grasp the world in it. Ideally it aims to make a perfect net. In order to make you totally secure, it would have to know everything. But it can't do this, if only because the net is not all that fine. Therefore, all sorts of things, good things or bad things, could slip through the net, so suddenly you would be surprised. Something more subtle could be caught in a finer net. Memory is limited in how fine a net it can make.

ME: Why?

DB: As I have just explained, one reason is that, though reality is always changing, memory has to fix certain things. Another reason is that it is based on abstraction. Whatever you remember is abstracted. You had your attention on a certain point when you remembered it. It attracted your attention; you thought about it; you were focusing on one problem and not another. So you were bound to be abstracting whatever you remembered. Therefore your memory must have left out a lot. In addition, it may not have been entirely correct, so it may not be right to use that pattern in a new situation. For example, we said in an earlier chapter that Mercator's projection is a good net near the equator, but it becomes an inadequate net near the poles; you need another net there. Thought then invents another net. Thought can invent more and more nets, with the aid of science and mathematics and so on, but it is always limited. What is most important in this context is that thought is not able to grasp in its net what is going on right now, at this very moment. It is true that in a certain area, thought can thus grasp movement. For example, with the aid of mathematics, we can predict the course of the planets, and we can control the trajectories of missiles. This is possible in general for things that are changing fairly regularly and not too rapidly. But we cannot predict or control the movement of the mind in this way, for this is far too subtle and complex and rapidly changing to be grasped by thought. Memory cannot hold in it the actual process by which the mind operates (including the response of the mind to memory itself).

ME: Besides, if you have an idea about the movement of the mind that you are watching, this will influence the whole process in a way that you cannot know beforehand.

DB: Moreover, it will also affect how you see it, and how you are disposed toward it, and how you feel about it. Equally important, it will influence the way you pay attention.

ME: That is very obvious in the political field where people are trying to solve problems. Because of the way they approach difficulties, they are inevitably going to distort how they see them.

DB: When you work with nature and material objects this can still happen, but at least you have your senses to tell you that it is not right. When it comes to more subtle things, like politics or emotions or your family or your philosophy, the senses won't tell you that you have gone wrong. You do not see the source of what has gone wrong; you only see the result. You try to deal with the result and not with the cause. But the attempt of the system to deal with the result can only confuse it more. We've got to get to the source.

We could make an image here of a stream that is being polluted. We could say that the memories are polluting our perception. Our perception is being polluted by wrong kinds of memories, such as memories of being hurt, memories of the necessity for giving supreme value to your country, memories of all the things you are used to, all the happiness you once had and can't have anymore, all of which prevent you from appreciating what is happening now. You can compare this to what happens in the stream. Every act of thought, every perception stirs up memories that enter near the source of the stream. People living downstream could say we've got a lot of pollution—let's make a plan to remove pollution from where we are. Not only does this not make sense, but also they might add a different kind of pollution in doing it. The thing to do is to go upstream and remove it there. That is really what we are after in this book. We want to get started moving upstream.

What people are doing in planting forests and saving the whales and so on is very necessary, and more of it should be done. Nevertheless it is still downstream. Unless something is done upstream, that is, in the process of thought, it won't really work in the long run. If it is done upstream, then what is being done downstream will make more sense. People haven't realized generally how thought is the source upstream; therefore, they are not really paying attention to the source.

ME: Could we perhaps look on all this as a wrong function of the brain?

DB: Yes. One could say that because of all the disturbance that we have described here, the brain has been excessively stirred up. The brain, being thus stirred up, requires some sort of order and security. But because the brain is not aware of the origin of its disturbance in memory, it tries inappropriately to correct this by dealing with it "downstream," that is, at the level of the content of thought and feelings, in which memory reveals itself.

The brain thus does not really know what the cause of the trouble is. Either it looks outward and says, for example, that a sense of security will come if I get more money, or else it looks inward and tries to find thoughts that will make it feel more secure. Neither of these approaches will deal properly with the memories that are disturbing the brain, however, and both will give rise to self-deception.

ME: But we are talking and thinking about all this right now. Not to be caught in self-deception as we do this requires perception, as we have already agreed. Where is this perception to come from?

DB: As we were saying in part I, thought cannot provide such perception. But we know that there is sense perception. We also suggested the possibility of perception through the mind, the ability to see that things are not coherent or the ability to get new ideas and so on, perhaps going on to insight. This suggests that the brain and the whole system may be able to act beyond dependence on memory. Now, there are two things that are clearly beyond memory. One is awareness, and the other is attention.

The word *awareness* is based on the same root as *wary* and *beware*, so that it suggests being watchful. "Be aware" doesn't mean just to think about it.

ME: It means a state of great energy and all your senses working very acutely.

DB: They are picking up all sorts of subtle cues.

ME: It is even more. You're taking in all the sounds, the sights, everything that is happening, and you are ready to look very closely at anything.

DB: That is to say, with the senses. Now let's look at what happens with the mind. If you knew that there might be a dangerous animal around, your senses would be very alert; you would pick up every cue. But also, you would be watching to see what all this might mean.

ME: The dangerous animal around here is thought! From realizing the meaning of this, an appropriate kind of awareness is generated, and this is really the seed of the solution to the problem.

DB: I think Krishnamurti put it very nicely when he said, "To live with thought [and by that he means the response of memory] is like living in a room with a poisonous snake." To do this, we've got to be very watchful. This snake image helps communicate what is meant by this awareness.

However, if we are not careful, this language can go too far and may lead us to dismiss the whole of thought as of little or no value. The kind of thought that we are talking about is that which is not aware of its origin in memory. Insofar as thought as a whole can become directly aware of its origin, it will not confuse its product with something independent of thought; all these problems will not take root. Indeed, when thoughts are very rational and orderly and the emotions are not too disturbed, we can in fact be at least somewhat aware of the origin of thought. One can then feel that one is thinking; one can tell that this thinking is affecting one's feeling. When it is very quiet one can sense that, and one can see relatively clearly what thought is doing within the overall operation of the mind.

ME: The problem is that we generally organize our lives so that there isn't much quietness. Is it somehow possible nevertheless to see the play of thought and emotion?

DB: To see this, you have to give your undivided attention to the process of thought, which, as we recall, includes the emotions along with the physical and chemical responses. The dominant feature of this process is the response of memory. As I said in part I, even the remembering of an emotion is actually an aspect of thought; it is not really an emotion, though it may seem like one. If you are aware, you can detect the difference between remembering an emotion and feeling an emotion directly because something has happened. This latter has a very different meaning.

ME: One of the differences would be the repetitive nature of "emotions" that are coming from memory.

DB: You can call them up again and again, if you wish.

ME: But in general, they just arise repetitively.

DB: The real emotion is not repetitive; it is constantly flowing. Therefore such an emotion might be a response to perception. And then you have to think about what it means, or maybe just let it go. In some way you could also say that a memory of thinking is actually just thought.

ME: What would be true thinking?

DB: Seeing something different. Working things out. Seeing what is not coherent. In the memory type of thought you are not very critical, and you just apply it automatically, in a kind of reflex action. But when you are really thinking, you are aware of any incoherence that there may be; for example, you may notice that there is something wrong here,

136

something needs attention. There is a very important difference, therefore, between thinking and thought.

I emphasize again that *thinking* is an active word — it is something actually going on — whereas thought means the reflexive activity of the residue of what has been done.

A great deal of our mental activity is just thought. Let's say that you have a prejudice that people of a certain race are inferior that has been given to you by somebody whom you trusted. It is on the memory disk. When you see members of this race, to you they *are* inferior. But you don't go through all the logic. The disk just works automatically and makes you *feel* their inferiority, so you immediately see them that way and are disposed to treat them as inferior.

Thinking might, however, question this reflexive activity by asking whether this thought is coherent, whether it really makes sense to act on such a basis.

ME: Questioning is a feature of thinking, whereas response from memory is thought.

DB: The first immediate response from memory clearly has no question in it. Krishnamurti used to give a nice example: if somebody asks your name, you tell him, and you don't have to stop to think. There is no question in there; it is clear that it comes from memory and just jumps into activity. Then suppose you get something a little more difficult, and you say, "I'm not sure; I've got to search my memory." If it gets still more difficult, you say, "I don't really know; maybe I should look it up in a book, or maybe somebody else knows." You are then beginning to consult the collective memory. At some stage you may say that nobody knows the answer. We have then to begin to think about it. For example, if something isn't working, we may say that we have a problem, which makes us think.

ME: What do you really mean here by a problem?

DB: When you accept something as a problem, you have implicitly thought of what you need as the solution, but you don't know how to get it. If you say that my problem is to get home, then I know where I want to get, but I just don't know the means. So the word *problem* suggests that we know the end but not the means. Suppose, however, that my problem is hurt. At first sight I seem to know the end, which may be that I want to get rid of the hurt. It appears that I just don't know the means, so I search for the means. But the answer to such a search would have to be contained in thought. And this thought would have to be rational and orderly. Yet we can see that the very existence of hurt distorts thought and enlists it in the service of continuing the hurt—for example, by justifying it through arguments that are self-deceptive. This kind of thought is just an extension of the very same process that produces and maintains the hurt, though this is hidden by our naming it as the means to end the hurt. We actually do not know the real nature of what we suppose to be the end, that is, getting rid of the hurt; therefore, our search for a means to do this is pointless.

The notion of a problem is useful when the thing with which we are dealing is not significantly affected by our thought about it, but not when, as with hurt, thought plays a crucial role in producing it. The notion of a problem is then too limited to be appropriate.

ME: Are you saying that this inquiry isn't limited?

DB: Yes. In other words, we are making a question, but we are not making a problem. In order to make a problem, I must say that I know what I want and that I must find the means. But with hurt we don't know quite what we are seeking to achieve. All that we really know about what is called the state of hurt is that things are not coherent.

ME: We can see some of the manifestations of incoherent thoughts. This gives a reflection of the source of the difficulty.

DB: We have proposed the idea that the source of this difficulty is memory, which seems reasonable. We are not even absolutely sure of that. That's what we do in any other area: we make a proposal, and we explore the proposal. We have given good reasons for saying that this could be the cause. So we say we don't know where memory is or what we have to do to get rid of its wrong action. We don't know the means, but as I've just said, we also really don't know the end. What is the end we are seeking? Of course, we want an orderly operation of memory; we don't want to get rid of memory—that's clear. That is to say, we want memory not to come in where it doesn't belong and not to muddle things up and not to give rise to incoherence. But we don't know what memory is or what makes it act, either coherently or incoherently.

ME: Yes. We want to end the incoherent response of memory, but we can't pursue this as a projected end, because to do so would be to assume that we know something which we really don't know.

DB: Yes, we don't really know just what the end is. If we start from this disorderly situation in memory and try to project what is to be meant by order from there, we are going to get lost. Suppose we say, "I'd like order in my life." So I look into my memory and ask, What does order mean? My memory may tell me that order means having nice rules, a good strong government—whatever it happens to mean according to my background, my memory. People once told me that order means such and such; I may accept it, or I may rebel against it. Thus, to me, order may mean dictatorship, and to another, order may be anarchy. Different memories control people's notions of order. I may say that I can put things in order on a line—I can order houses or the streets—but to order the mind, I really don't know what that means.

ME: Psychological order is going to be of a different kind anyway—much more subtle. So this brings us back to the nature of perception. Are you saying that order would come if we were to be open to perception?

DB: To go into this, let's come back to attention, which is a key part of perception. We go from awareness to attention. In a way attention brings it all together. The word *attention* means literally to stretch the mind toward something. *Tension* means "stretch" and *a* means "toward." The two words *attention* and *intention* are closely related. According to your attention, your intention will develop. If you don't pay attention to something, you cannot have an appropriate intention toward it. Such attention then turns to intention, and this intention turns to further action. You can then think of perception bringing things in through the senses and so on through awareness, coming to attention, and—somehow in a way we don't understand—coming back to intention and action, and then to perception, awareness, and attention again, in a sort of spiraling cycle.

ME: We were just using the word *order*. Can you say more about what this means?

DB: We have to be able to leave the meaning of a word somewhat open. As in a map, we cannot get a complete covering of the territory. The word *order*, whatever it may happen to mean to us, cannot cover all that it could mean. The meaning may have to be extended. In general, meanings should be capable of extension; otherwise, we cannot communicate properly.

ME: It goes against a great deal of our culture to say that meanings should be capable of being extended in this way.

DB: But actually we are always doing it, although we generally don't notice it. You must find the right degree of fixity of meaning; you must hold meanings to some extent, but they must be open to further extensions. More generally, we have to have an attitude to language as being open. In poetry you can see that it is more open. To be sure, in certain areas, such as science and technology, one does find that clarity often calls for a fairly literal use of language. But more generally, clarity is not necessarily the same as a perfectly literal description. Indeed, absolutely literal use of language would make it rigid and dead.

In science and technology, you also have to leave things open to allow for the exploration of something new. For example, when the field of mechanics was set up, they changed the meaning of words; *energy*, for instance, was given a different meaning from that which it had in ordinary life. There was a long period when they had to give meanings to other words as well. So even in science, we have to be open to extending the meaning; otherwise, communication will be very restricted.

ME: Is this approach to meaning part of what is to be signified as perception?

DB: Yes. For the perception of meaning is in fact the basic mental perception. Thus, to say, "I see what you mean," is the same as to say, "I understand what you mean." It does not signify that I remember what you mean.

ME: I *feel* that we are sharing something.

DB: But does that mean that we can see that it is the same as something we once knew in the past? Or does it mean that it is something new we have shared at this moment?

ME: I mean that we understand something that we perceive together in the same sort of way at the same time.

DB: We didn't perceive it before in just that way. The fundamental perception at this subtle level is to perceive new meaning.

140

Meaning is in general something that you can't put your finger on; that is, you can't make it manifest. The coarse net of thought can only perceive rather unsubtle meanings. We can put the subtler meanings into thought after we perceive them, but unless we allow the significance of words to be extensible, we are stuck in our rigid meanings.

ME: It might be that more poetic language has to be used at this level.

DB: There needs to be more free use of language at the very least. One could discuss this at great length, but I don't think that is our purpose in this book. We just want to make our attitude clear here.

Attention is stretching the mind toward something, and that is part of perceiving the meaning. You are trying to perceive the whole meaning. Attention is something with no limit to its possible subtlety; I think attention could make finer nets without limit. We may, however, direct our attention by thought: for example, by saying, "Look at this, think about this." In this way we could limit the fineness of our net, and we generally do in fact. But attention is potentially capable of unlimited fineness of net, of unlimited subtlety. However, it takes high energy to be very subtle and fine.

ME: Most of our energies seem to be dissipated in the conflict that has arisen from this process of thought having gone wrong. This is a vicious circle that requires clarity in the first place—it requires an insight into this process to start with. So we seem to be stuck.

DB: But not really. For from this more subtle mind new intentions can flow out, new actions, new ways of thinking, and our thoughts will begin to change too. Therefore thoughts may eventually be able to move out of this trap that they are in—in which the system does not realize what the source of thought is and treats everything that happens as if it were independent of memory and thought. What we need is a kind of attention that is subtle enough to see how thought is working. And, as has been said many times throughout this book, what is meant by thought is the whole response of memory, including feeling, muscular tension, emotional excitation, and so on.

We have just been giving some attention to how language works, and to how meanings work. All this has to be attended to, and ordinarily we don't do it. We have in this way to see very deeply and broadly how thought is affecting things. Our culture has developed the notion that thought has in itself no effect, that it simply tells you something and then vanishes. But as we have been saying, it doesn't vanish, and its residue in memory has all sorts of effects on the emotions, on the body, on relationships, and on whatever anybody does. As we have also been saying, we meet all these effects, and then thought comes up and treats them as if they were independent. In doing this, it generally doesn't go through the thinking process but is just disposed to respond automatically. In a certain sense, thoughts may therefore be said to *think us*, because thoughts may produce the impressions that we have not only about others but also about ourselves; for example, I'm this sort of person, I feel that way, because I always did—it goes back to the way I was treated from very early in my life, and so on.

ME: Thought is most of the time in operation in people's lives, and while it is in operation it is obscuring this more subtle process unless there is attention given to the operation of thought. Is attention an activity in the brain?

DB: We don't know—it obviously affects the brain profoundly. This raises the question that Krishnamurti asked, Is the brain all there is, or is there something beyond the brain? Is there a mind that is too subtle to be comprehended within the framework of the idea of the brain? Brain function could become more and more subtle or refined and so on, and at some stage you might wonder if it is the brain as such, or is there something beyond?

It would be wrong for us to answer this question, because we don't know the answer. But it is important for us to entertain the question. For merely to have that question causes our thought to hold back, to give pause, and to be somewhat tentative and fluid, rather than to be absolutely certain and rigid. To be sure, most scientists seem to believe that the brain is all that is significant in this context. But in fact nobody really knows. It wouldn't be right, for example, to presuppose that science already has, or even that it ultimately will have, a net fine enough to grasp everything important about the brain and the mind. There is indeed a tendency for science to go too far in making presuppositions of this kind. The key point is not to discuss whether or not we know the answer to this particular question; rather, it is that by asking this general kind of question seriously we are suspending a great deal of irrelevant activity of thought and are having a beneficial effect on the brain by doing so.

ME: Many people say that there is nothing beyond thought, let alone nothing beyond the brain.

DB: Yes, but how do they know that? Let us now come back to the question of awareness and attention. Suppose I say, "Let's pay attention." Do I mean that we should think? Implicitly everybody knows there is something beyond thought, not only sense perception (with which people would evidently have to agree) but also something more subtle.

ME: I was talking about the assumptions that people make explicitly. Assumptions can override what you know implicitly.

DB: That's the whole way memory works. It imposes its pattern on experience, and you don't see it happening; therefore, you say that must be the way it is. But I think if you just stop and question it, you can see that when you say that one is to pay attention, you do not mean that one is to think. Thus, if you ask me to give attention to what is in the room, I could close my eyes and think about what is in the room. But to do this would make no sense. To pay attention means, first of all, to be open to the senses. However, it signifies much more than that. It signifies being open to seeing the meaning of it all. I can't really just say I already know the meaning and that I therefore just have to think from what I know. Indeed, if I knew what everything means, then there would be no need to pay attention to the meaning. So I think that in this sense everybody implicitly accepts that paying attention is more than thought, and is more subtle than thought, and is not based solely on memory. "Pay attention" means that something is going on right now and that you should be observing it and not forcing it to conform to a pattern based on memory.

ME: Thought then scans it, and in this way it becomes memory.

DB: Also attention may scan it in an infinitely subtle way. The whole point is that at any given moment, thought is limited in its subtlety, if only because it is based on what we know. As I have already suggested, scientists may assume that in essence they already know at least the general lines of everything that is significant. But if you stop to think about it, you will see that there is no foundation in fact for saying this. Though it has no foundation in fact, to make such an assumption may make one feel better, may give one a sense of security. But in fact one purchases this sense of security at the expense of disrupting the operation of the brain.

As we have already said many times, the right operation of the brain is not to make such an assumption but to question and to suspend the activity of thought enough to allow you to give attention to whatever may be relevant. If, for example, you have an assumption about somebody, you are not likely to pay much attention to that person. Thus, if you pass a man in the street you know very well, you may hardly notice him. You could say that you saw him, but if you are asked what he was wearing—you don't know. You weren't paying attention; you were seeing him through your memory. A few tiny little things you saw; the rest was memory. We wouldn't attempt to drive a car that way. You must pay attention to what is on the road, not just to what you remember. With human relationships we tend to behave as if we didn't have to give such attention and could just operate from the response of memory. But in the long run, it is even more dangerous to do this with human relationships than to drive a car without paying attention.

ME: And certainly with political relationships it becomes yet more crucial.

DB: So we are caught in responding from memory and seeing in terms of memory without knowing that this is actually happening. Our perceptions are shaped and colored by memory in a way of which we are not conscious, along with our dispositions and actions and intentions and so on. This approach evidently leads to irrelevant actions and ultimately to conflict. Our intentions are then also irrelevant and conflicting because we are not actually in contact with what is there.

As an example of this sort of thing, one can consider that when they first showed films in the American West, the cowboys were so carried away by the film that they would shoot at the villain. The point is that they were taking an irrelevant action aimed at stopping his villainy. For, if you want to do this, you should turn off the projector rather than shoot at the screen. In that case there were no serious consequences, but there could be serious consequences very easily. Suppose there is a man you regard as an enemy, and you feel that you have to stop him by shooting him. But why is he your enemy in the first place? Because of thoughts. So you are caught up in a response from memory, which is generally not relevant.

ME: You could give the example of Russia and America. For over seventy years, there existed a state of severe tension and hostility between these two countries, which gave rise to a persistent danger of nuclear war. It seems that over this long period of time there was a tacit agreement between America and Russia that they were in conflict and that they operated from this agreement.

DB: They had different aims and purposes, and they acted as if they were independent, but in fact they are mutually dependent. And if one had attempted to defeat the other, they would have destroyed the world. So the whole thing has no meaning.

ME: What you are saying is this: such a situation arises because thought isn't in direct contact with reality.

DB: The basic difficulty, as I pointed out earlier, is that thought is not in contact with the fact that conflict between the two sides is ultimately a product of thought itself and is not something that arises independently of thought. Thus, the nations of America and Russia, along with the idea that they have supreme value to their respective citizens, were produced by thought in the way that we talked about in chapter 1. So also were capitalism and communism, with people thinking that these mutually exclusive sets of values were of overriding importance, so that everything could be destroyed to defend them. To be sure, this particular conflict between America and Russia is now much less intense, so that this particular danger of war seems to have receded. But then, because thought still generally confuses its own product with a reality independent of thought, new conflicts of a similar nature will have indeed already arisen, and more will inevitably arise as a result of differences in thought about religion, race, economic rivalries, and perhaps further questions to which thought may give supreme importance in the future. To bring about a resolution of such conflicts, each side has sooner or later to meet the thought of the other. In doing this, both sides will have to be ready to question their basic ideas, to examine them, and to change them to be more in accord with reality.

ME: If one imagines a world that is less sharply divided by national boundaries, a world in which such communication could take place, isn't it possible that there will be a move toward a kind of world totalitarian state? I think that people would be wary of this. How ever bad national-ism is, it could be worse if there were one government governing the whole world and that government were tyrannical.

DB: Nationalism can be very bad; a single government ruling the world might also be bad. But I think that unless we clear up thought, everything is ultimately going to be bad. I think that in the same way the interna-tional government could make its own kind of muddle. Nationalism was originally a move against smaller divisions. They overcame smaller divisions and produced different ones, and internationalism will produce further divisions between people in yet a different way. Unless thought begins to operate in a coherent manner (which requires that people be aware of and understand how they confuse the effects of memory with independent reality) then, as I have already explained, it is all going to come out more or less the same in the long run.

In general we do need to have some kind of international government, but we also need local governments. Thus, as I have said earlier, nations could function as convenient units for people sharing a common culture and other interests of various kinds. But in all this, we need the principle that no government is supreme.

The real question is not to take one direction or the other. What is needed is to get to the source of this muddle and not to try to clear it up downstream. This requires attention to thought and to the whole process of thought, which includes feeling, desire, will, intention, and muscular tension, going yet further out into the society. For thought is communicated between people; it is much more collective than individ-ual, through language and television and radio and so on.

ME: You used a metaphor earlier on about a polluted river—is it possible to go beyond the point where the river is being polluted? I'm questioning whether we could arrive at a subtler level of intelligence.

DB: I think that we can. With attention becoming more and more subtle, we are moving upstream, and eventually we may in this way be carried beyond the "pollution." Intelligence may thus be able to perceive and act in a way that is not limited or conditioned by the pollution. At present the thought process profoundly affects the whole mind in a destructive way, because it imposes all sorts of irrelevant emotions and desires and assumptions and distorted facts, leading to illusion. The

146

whole system gets disrupted—it doesn't even work in a proper way physically and chemically. But is there a subtler movement of intelligence that is not affected by this and that can begin to reach below or deeper than the pollution—something more fundamental than the pollution?

We have then to ask what we mean by intelligence. As I've said elsewhere, it is often useful to look into the derivation of words, even though the original meaning may not be exactly what it is now, because to do this gives insight into the archaeology of the thought process. By knowing how the words have developed, we understand their whole meaning better. Also people in early days when they coined the words may have had a fresher perception, less based on routine ways of using language. Our present meanings are often rather habitual, dull, and mechanical. To look at the roots of the words helps us to get out of this.

The word *intelligence* is based on a Latin root, *intelligere*, which in turn is based on two words: *inter* and *legere*. *Legere* might mean "to choose" or "to gather"—you could say that it means to choose between. The word *collect* means "to gather together," "to choose together"; and *select*, "to gather or choose apart." Thought selects and collects—it selects things into categories. It selects them apart and collects them together according to their differences and similarities, but also according to a pattern that memory imposes. In other words, you know how to select and collect more or less from memory. However, with intelligence you gather things from in between—you don't use the old categories. You could say that it is like reading between the lines. It makes new categories. In this way at least, intelligence is a process that is not limited by memory but has a perceptive movement. It can perceive afresh what is the right way to put things together—what is the right way to select and collect. It can give rise to new ways of doing this that are between the old ways and can go beyond them. So with intelligence we don't stick to extremes of saying either us or them, good or bad, America or Russia—we can be in between, and we can go beyond into new ways. Sticking to the extremes, the process that comes from memory, is rigid.

The word *intellect* is the past participle of the word *intelligere*. At this rate, intellect is what *has been* chosen or gathered, just as thought is what one *has been* thinking. Intellect is therefore what is on the disk. It acts like a program, and it works. In this way, everything can be organized logically, but it basically is not new. It is therefore always limited, according to what you happen to have learned, what the society happens to have learned, and so on. Therefore, though intellect is useful and necessary, it is not the whole story. If we attempt to make it so, intellect will go wrong, for the same reason that thought has generally gone wrong.

To sum up, then, we need a kind of intelligence that goes beyond thought, that is not based on memory and is more subtle than memory. It is a perceptive activity that collects and selects in new ways. And in doing this, it gives rise to new meanings. For the ways in which we put things together and keep them apart constitute a key part of what they mean. And according to what they mean is how you behave and how you are.

But of course some things may interfere with this. Memory may put the brain into a wrong chemical state, so that it can't respond properly to this intelligence. It may be too disturbed neurophysiologically and also affected by the wrong neurochemicals, arising, for example, in very powerful anger or fear or anxiety, or even pleasure.

In our society, people are generally not in the right state to respond to intelligence, except perhaps occasionally when they are either very quiet or very deeply interested for the moment, so that all this other content is set aside. But we urgently need to have a sustained intelligence, not just an occasionally active intelligence. A sustained intelligence would allow creativity to operate.

This intelligence is what really makes it possible to change things. It changes them upstream at the source; then the change works its way downstream. Awareness, attention, and some thinking are needed. Indeed, we've got to think clearly and accurately about our process of thought, and this too can help lead us upstream into intelligence. Clearly passion is also needed, energy. However, the intelligence will liberate energy, because we are wasting it now in all this chaotic movement of thought.

ME: This picture still doesn't convey clearly enough the means by which one could go about doing this. I see that it is imperative that this kind of intelligence be given a chance to operate. I think we ought to go into how or what one should do or not do in order to bring this about.

DB: We could first bring in here what Krishnamurti said, that you might begin by bringing order into your daily life, especially by noticing all the disorder in relationships through looking without judgment at what you are actually doing. This would help to bring your mind into a more orderly, quiet state, a state more conducive to intelligence. So that is one thing you can do—become aware of the general disorder in your thoughts and in your daily life. It is not a matter of repetitious practice, but rather of doing it from moment to moment; it has to be something that is constantly fresh and creative. You can't make a rule about how to do that. These are some of the things you can do downstream that can help you move upstream.

In this observation, it is necessary to be aware of the overall process of thought, as well as its detailed content. What is called for here is not a set of exercises, in the sense that you should repeat them mechanically to obtain a certain result. Nevertheless, there are things you can do that help you to become attentive and aware, through seeing what happens while you are doing them, for the sake of learning and not for the sake of getting a result. One is to pay special attention to the general process in which thought and feeling are related together through memory and its response. For example, a certain thought may disturb us, and later this disturbance reaches the solar plexus or the abdomen. We then say that we have got a deep gut feeling; we take this as proof that it is right. But in fact it may be a mechanical response to memory—just an extension of the thought process. The disturbing thought may have done it. If you regard it as having come up independently, you'll give it very great value and will be caught up in it. It is very important to pay attention to where these things come from, so that they will be given their proper value.

ME: So the emphasis here is really on *looking*.

DB: Yes. But you also have to have some notion of what to look at. One thing I suggest that one can do is to use words in a certain way to help make it clear how thought and feeling are actually related. To bring out what I mean here, let me begin by pointing out that ordinarily we use words to talk *about* a subject. Thus, if I say that I am angry, I am talking *about* my state of mind. However, this may be very misleading. For when I say that I am angry, this generally tends to fix that state of mind (which might otherwise, as in a very young child, change fairly rapidly of its own accord). So these words are participating significantly in sustaining the whole process (though thought does not in general notice this).

Let me emphasize this point by saying once again that ordinarily we use words to talk *about* something. I am proposing instead that we use words to call up and sustain that very thing, so that it actually takes place in our minds. Instead of thinking *about anger*, what is being called for then is to *think anger*.

For example, suppose there was an incident that made me angry. After a while, I may calm down, but the anger will still be there, perhaps simmering in the background. My suggestion is then *intentionally* and *seriously* to think the thoughts that bring out and sustain the anger that is present in the background. (For example, "He treated me outrageously; he pushed me around; he acted in an unforgivable way.") If you do this, you will notice that the feelings of anger surge up with much greater strength, thus clearly demonstrating a close connection between words and feelings (such as anger). Vice versa, you will notice also a feeling of pressure, an impulse to keep on thinking along the general line of thought needed to maintain your anger. You will find it hard to give up such thoughts, because it will then seem that you do indeed have a valid reason to be angry.

ME: Yet, when you think about it more carefully, there doesn't seem to be a good reason. There seems just to be an emotional reason. As has been said, the heart has its reasons. If you've been hurt, you often don't want to remember that hurt, but it keeps impinging, whether you want it or not. Generally you feel that there is no value in that at all, because you want to get on with life, and you don't want that memory of suffering and unhappiness to interfere. But it comes in anyway. I don't know if there is an answer to why it comes in, but it seems to be like a record that keeps playing.

DB: If we didn't have this interference by memory, we could conclude that our feelings may in general be telling us something valid to which we have to pay serious attention. As I have suggested in part I, in early times they probably more or less worked in that way. With civilization came a great many "disks" that produce conglomerate, memory-based feelings that have no meaning, that we don't even want, that we know are interfering with everything we do want, and that are making us do wrong, destructive things. What are we going to do with these feelings? Are we going to suppress them, deny that we have them? Or shall we carry them out? Whatever we do along these lines doesn't really work. So we are somehow making a serious mistake.

In some cases where feelings are true feelings, we can indeed say that it is right that the heart has its reasons. If there is such a feeling that we should do something, then that is a good reason. But when we have these mechanical feelings from the "disks," we give them the same value. Thus one may be led to say, "I don't see a good reason to be angry, but I feel a good reason to be angry." In fact, however, my reason very often nevertheless tells me that I shouldn't be angry; it would be better not to be. Yet the emotion doesn't go away, as it normally should when reason says that it is not in proportion to the actual situation.

You could perhaps say, however, that anger could sometimes be appropriate if it came in a short burst just to let another person know that he or she is doing something that is causing you trouble. But then, if it doesn't work in that short burst, it's going to go wrong. For to keep it going, you will have to accept that you have a valid reason to be angry. It will then build up, and thought will be distorted; you're then liable to do something that you may regret. You may hurt somebody, who may never forgive you. In this way, anger can build up into terrible things if you sustain it. Going from that short outburst of anger to sustained anger is the crucial mistake. Therefore, thought, which is responsible for this, really has no place in anger.

You can begin to pay attention to all this, and as you do so, you will begin to see how the whole process is working. You can in this way get an actual feeling for how the thought is giving rise to and sustaining anger and how anger is sustaining that thought. It's a movement from two sides in which you are trapped. To sense this movement properly, you have to be, as it were, on a "knife edge" between being "carried away" by the feelings of anger and losing awareness of what is happening and avoiding or otherwise "escaping" these feelings (by denying that they are there, for example). If you can stay near this unstable "midpoint," you can then begin to be aware of the overall movement of memory as it works. It is then possible for the overall process to start to correct this disharmony in the thought process, the origin of which is that thought generally doesn't see its source in memory.

ME: It is interesting that you say that it is the overall process that corrects the disharmony, implying that is not your intentional action aimed at a defined end. Could you go into this further?

DB: I would say that it is the overall action of the whole mind and heart that corrects this disharmony. One reason why the word *you* is inappropriate here is that the word *I* (and therefore also *you*) is very unclear and ambiguous in its meaning. Thus, you usually identify yourself with the body, and in this case, you end with the skin. However, if a blind man is tapping a stick and he holds it tightly, he feels that he ends at the end of the stick, where the connection to the room is loose. If he holds the stick loosely, he feels that he ends at his fingers.

ME: Yes. If you're driving a car, you feel the boundary is the outside of the car.

DB: A boundary is established wherever the connection is loose. That sort of boundary is valid. But you may think that you are further inside your body and may therefore also feel that you end further inside. Or you may extend to the boundary of your country, so that whoever crosses that boundary is felt to be attacking you. Or you could go on and say that you are the whole universe. Or similarly, you could say that you are a manifestation of the whole universe.

Along the same lines, I may say that inside me is an observer who sees this chair as fairly separate, because the connection between us is loose. But if I look at my feelings, I see that this sort of description would be mistaken, because my thought is participating significantly in producing and sustaining those feelings. Therefore between my thought and my feelings is a tight connection. It is thus a mistake to say that I am an observer who is observing and possibly controlling an anger that is separate from me. I *am* the anger that I observe, and therefore it has no meaning for me to try to control it; it is just one process. I need a subtler intelligence involving the whole system that doesn't start from such a false separation. It is a rather crude kind of thought that separates them.

ME: Because it's so pervasive it doesn't appear to be crude.

DB: This kind of division is, as I have already said, valid in certain cases, but in other cases, such as the one I have just described, I see that it makes no sense. Therefore, I have to go beyond the crude kind of operation of thought that divides itself from the anger that it arouses and sustains. But thought cannot itself find any means to end this false process, because it is based on something like a program in the memory. This compels it to go on rigidly with the assumption of a sharp, fixed sort of division between itself and such feelings. However, as explained earlier, there is an intelligence that doesn't divide falsely into rigidly fixed categories. When this intelligence is awakened, the system works as a whole, and the thought process can be freed from these irrelevant and destructive "programs." It need then no longer go on with meaningless responses, such as trying to overcome anger with a demand from the intellect, while it at the same time is committed to going on with anger in order to satisfy an emotional demand.

The reason this sort of disharmony between emotion and intellect arises is basically that, as has been suggested earlier, memory interferes with the natural relationship between the two (which, as we recall, should properly take place through the thick bundle of nerves connecting the two respective centers of the brain). Memory has been built up over the ages, so that within it is firmly imprinted this sharp, fixed distinction between thought and feeling. It is on the "disk" of practically everybody, in such a way that it tends to spring into action very rapidly in response to whatever may happen. In order to be free of this response, we have to have the possibility for the mind to see something as it is happening *immediately*, rather than waiting for memory to filter it, to select, collect, order, and arrange it into previously determined categories. What does it mean to see it or perceive it as it happens? It means that thought is aware of itself in its own movement as the body is aware of itself in its own movement, without any sense of a separate observer. So when thought takes place, somehow the whole system will know that what happens is the result of memory.

In such observation and awareness, various feelings will come up. If you're really able to watch the whole process from moment to moment, you'll not only sense these feelings, but you will also sense how they give rise to further thoughts. Through attention of this kind, you'll get a sense of how it all happens, and you will be able to see that it is all one process, but that this process does not have a great deal of significance. For if you get a conglomerate, memory-based feeling coming out of thought, it evidently doesn't mean very much. In this way one sees one's anger is not all that significant; therefore, it will cease. But if one thinks that one has a valid reason to be angry, because, for example, someone has acted outrageously and unforgivably, it will never cease. That reason is constantly springing up as the "disk" of memory operates, and the whole process then affects the emotions. It's like the weather. It's a kind of emotional weather.

As I have already indicated, when one sees that this sort of response doesn't have much significance, it generally goes away. But that's not our primary objective, to make it go away — the main point is to *see*. If we made it go away this time without seeing how it all works, it would come back next time.

What I have been saying gives an example of the kind of thing that is called for. The more subtle intelligence, being awakened, will not only be able to deal with responses such as anger but also with what is encountered when we go into human relationships and politics and so on. The attempt to solve the environmental, social, cultural (and ultimately political) problem on the basis of the crude and fragmented structure of thought that is now common will never work. It needs the subtle intelligence that is an undivided whole. Getting to the root of the "pollution" then leads eventually to going beyond that root and reaching the unpolluted source of this intelligence. And that in itself begins to clean up the pollution, rather as certain bacteria can do in a river.

Chapter 4

ILLUSION AND REALITY

MARK EDWARDS: From what we have been talking about, it seems to me that thought has produced a world pervaded with illusory features, but that, as we have been saying, this overall process actually produces real results. The process of thought is, in this way, extremely vulnerable to self-deception.

Could we discuss the actual reality that is behind the illusions of the world generated by thought?

DAVID BOHM: For the sake of general coherence, I think that we do have to make the assumption that whatever we know or think about is part of a more fundamental and broader actual reality that is not generated by thought. We have been saying that thought doesn't cover everything; it is limited. Therefore, whatever we know of the world, there is always more. We find things that we didn't know about, and we find things that contradict what we already know. This is a sign of reality that is beyond our knowledge, our will, our intention, and our desire, as well as being beyond what we have created. The feeling that has arisen from the consideration of all this is that we exist in a vast, illimitable reality out of which we emerged, probably, as suggested by scientific evidence, through a process of evolution. But, of course, religious people say it came from God. Whichever assumption we make, we are here in this reality; we are participating in it.

To what extent have we created this reality, and to what extent has thought contributed to it? It is clear that the reality of society has been

155

made largely by us. However, nature was in the first instance created by its own process. The planets and so on—all of that was created before we even got here. We then began to make a society and, as has been said in part I, the rules of that society were made by us, through our thinking, along with the institutions, the roads, the farms, and the factories. Most of what we see around us was thus made by us, physically, culturally, institutionally, and socially, through our language and our communications.

Nevertheless, when we look at society, we often get the feeling that it wasn't made by us—thus, the poet A. E. Housman's "I, a stranger and afraid/In a world I never made." That's an illusion. Although I personally didn't make it, all of us together, including our ancestors, somehow did make it. It came about through a historical process. But this reality that was made by us was, as I have already said, given shape by thought. Moreover, we are even now contributing to the process by unwittingly subscribing to this general pattern of thought.

It is clear then that although the ground of reality does not depend on our thought, nevertheless a certain part of reality is the result of thought. Insofar as our thought leads to actions that cohere with this reality, whether generated by thought or not, it can be regarded as correct. For example, if our thought says that certain things should happen, and they actually do happen, we say that it is giving us a good picture of reality, a good representation. Otherwise, we say that it is not good and that we should change it. And we can reasonably expect our thought to change in this way, because not only the reality that is independent of thought but even the reality that we made through thought contains things we never expected. For example, we intended merely to make industry grow, but in doing this we also made pollution and environmental degeneration. Indeed, the reality that we make through thought is seldom, if ever, what such thought leads us to expect. We need our attention and perception to keep on watching it, so that our thought keeps up with the reality. If our thought is too rigid, it won't do so. If our minds were alive and alert, we would notice this very quickly and start to change our thought. The point is that, for reasons that we have been discussing, we don't change easily. Instead, we hold on to our thought and defend it against evidence that it should change, and in this way we begin to create illusion. The word *illusion* basically means playing false, and it implies that we are creating a representation of reality that is not coherent with reality as a whole. Thus stage magicians create illusion by leading you to think differently about what is happening. Their first point is to get you by their patter not to pay attention to what is actually happening but to concentrate on what they are saying instead. Meanwhile, they switch something, and the result looks like magic. In other words, if it really happened the way they say it did, it would have been magic, but actually, they have created an illusion of magic. Thus rabbits would seem to have emerged from a hat that never went into the hat. In fact, however, you know that the rabbit went into the hat while your attention was directed elsewhere.

This is really the basic trick by which thought creates illusion. Indeed, inherent in memory is such a possibility to create illusion. The key point here is that memory is something you never see. I may remember something, but I don't know where this memory is. I may say that I recall, I recollect, but that only takes some bits out of the content of memory and puts them together into an image, a picture, a description. I don't perceive where it all came from. Moreover, as we've seen in earlier chapters, memory responds to whatever happens by just springing into action. In doing this it infuses my perception, but I don't see that this is a result of the operation of memory. Memory has in this way been interchanged with perception. It may have come in too fast to be seen as such, or else in some other way to which I wasn't able to pay attention. When I do get to look at the results, thought then says that they are something independent; it is not the action of memory, but it is what I actually perceive.

The magician is thus reality imitating thought. Indeed, thought has been doing this ever since it began. It has a tendency to fall into such a process, and then it gets worse. Some of the things that you remember contain very high emotional values, and they are presented as real, and independent of thought, so that you may want to defend them. If you had some actual reality of very high value, it would be quite reasonable to do this. Suppose, however, that you have the memory that you are a great person. This produces a great feeling. But then somebody says no, you're an idiot. The memory of what an idiot is then comes up, and that feels very unpleasant. So it shakes you badly inside. The body objects — it doesn't know that this is just memory, and it gives signals to the effect that one doesn't want to be shaken up like this. The thought process then says that this is no good and asks how it can stop the disturbance.

So it calls on memory. And, as I explained in part I, memory, like the computer disk, supplies an immediate answer. It may say, "I am not an idiot, I deny it; somebody else is the idiot." In this way, I substitute somebody else for myself. This is a trick that is on my disk. Suddenly the whole thing is gone, and the body feels better. In that way I can create illusion. First there was the illusion that I am very great and wonderful; second, the other person began to create the illusion that I am an idiot; and then I created the illusion that the other person is the idiot.

ME: That's a very intense process that is charged with great emotion and with a strong sense of reality, which makes it hard to observe without distortion.

DB: You identify the content of your thought about yourself with your actual being. Either implicitly or explicitly it refers to what you are. If I say, "I am an idiot," this refers to me. If I identify with my country and my country is wrong, this means that I am wrong. If I say my family, it may also mean that I am wrong, because it reflects on me. So I get really physically disturbed, and I come to believe that I am under attack. I then begin to defend myself against evidence that something may be wrong with those thoughts of mine that have to do with myself. This brings me to subvert thought altogether, as thought that defends itself against evidence that it may be wrong is worse than useless. It creates illusion and leads us astray.

ME: Politicians in power tell us that we have never had it so good, and those trying to get into government tell us that we have never had it so bad. They interpret the facts in the way that suits them best. This is evidently a very serious problem with the process of thought. Indeed, it probably gets very close to one of the most destructive manifestations of the disorder in thought. We have already alluded to an example of this in previous chapters: I have seen the extraordinary extent to which people are prepared to adapt to the most terrible living conditions and still hold on to the beliefs and ideas that are dear to them but that inevitably trap them in extreme poverty and distress.

DB: It is implied in such behavior that people have identified certain things as the very essence of themselves, and that these things therefore have to be defended at all costs. We don't know what the self is. No one has seen it. Maybe we do have a self—a deep self—who knows? But most of what we call the self is actually thought identifying certain qualities with what one is: I'm great, I'm wonderful, I'm very competent, highly extraordinary, and so on. Or if you can't maintain the notion that you are great and wonderful, you may soon come to the opposite thought, identifying yourself as terrible, a wicked sinner. But ultimately this becomes the same process.

ME: The most persistent idea we have is that the self isn't just thought.

DB: We don't know if it is or it isn't—we may have a self that is more. Most of what we call the self is the response of memory that fills the brain, and this self is, of course, just the result of thought. But even if there is a true self beyond this, we're not going to be able to see it as long as we are so confused about it. I like to use here the analogy of Las Vegas. You could say that while all the lights in that city are shining so brightly, you can't see the universe. There is a universe, but you can't see it. Indeed, you could readily assume that the universe is Las Vegas. It would be a very strange universe, but it would be what you actually saw. If anybody talked about stars, you might then say that if we can't see them, it's just empty talk. But if you could turn off those lights and stop all that noise, then the true universe would begin to show. So maybe we have a true self, or maybe the self is part of the universe as a whole. Perhaps there is some true being, but it doesn't show through all this superficial noise and flashing light that civilization has built up.

ME: I'm keen to go more deeply into this tendency of thought to defend itself against evidence that it is incorrect. This surely is a terribly dangerous quality. It's not giving us straight information, and even in the face of evidence that we might be wrong, we are going to go on defending ideas with which we have identified in the past (and I suppose our self has become composed partly of such ideas). It would be like saying that I've generally avoided seeing that I've been wrong. To be sure, I do change my thoughts occasionally, but only to form eventually another rigid view that is also ultimately wrong.

DB: This is a process of identification with ideas. For example, if a boy is called a bad boy for long enough, he finally identifies himself as being a bad boy, and he is that bad boy from then on. People get identified very early in life with certain things, and it's hard for them to get out

159

of that identification. The identity is not merely the idea abstractly, but the feeling, the desire, the urge; it's a tremendous neurophysiological process. Through the sense of necessity of defending the identity at all costs, one gets caught up in self-deception. So people are generally not at all clear on the question of identity and thought.

ME: Why do you think that there is this tendency to want to identify with something else, with a collective of some kind? Where do you think that comes from?

DB: It must have been there very early. During most of human evolution people were part of a group of twenty to forty and probably felt very close to it. Outside of it, they might have felt rather isolated and anxious, as well as in real danger. Similarly, in some sense we still really need to be part of something larger, some sort of culture and society. I think that the question should instead be, Why does this give rise to a false process, to self-deception? We would not object to needing to be part of something larger if it didn't give rise to all this self-deception.

I think there must be something wrong with this process, at least as it has developed in civilized society. Civilized society currently encourages people to think of themselves as individuals, but it also attacks them as individuals. It says they're weak, they're nothing, and it asks them, Who do you think you are? It says, You're nothing, just little you. At the same time it is implicit that to do this is wrong, that there should be something more to life than that. You can't fill your consciousness with little me, if only because it's not interesting. It's also insecure. If I'm so small, anything could happen to me. I need something bigger, stronger, more interesting. Therefore I may imagine, simply assume, that I've got it by saying I belong to my country, my family, my friends, my business, and that in this way I have an identity. But actually I invent such an identity. Because that identity itself is shaky, I'll have to keep on defending the ideas that are behind it, deceiving myself. If I identify with my country and I discover that my country is corrupt, weak, and stupid, that would mean that I am that way too. I could disidentify, but then I would have to ask, Who am I? But instead, I say, That's wrong; my country is great. Thus I create an illusion.

In this sort of way, people feel the need for finding an identity by thought and thereafter defending it against evidence that it may not be what they thought it was. If we had a true identity, that is, true being, why would we ever have to defend it in this way? You would just say, "That's what I am." It is only because I suspect that I do not have a true identity that I may be driven into this foolish activity of defending the essential qualities that are supposed to make up my identity against evidence that they are not as I think they are. If I had a true identity, nothing that anybody said could take it away from me.

ME: In the eyes of society, each one of us is in fact rather insignificant and small.

DB: Yes, and each one of us supports this idea by thinking that way. But it may not be true at all. Maybe we're making ourselves insignificant and small by believing that we are. Our society, in order to stabilize itself, leads us to believe in that sort of idea. There is a fear that otherwise we would get to be too "uppity" and a bit difficult to control. A few people are allowed to think otherwise — great leaders, charismatic figures, recognized geniuses, and so on — but ordinary people are not allowed to do this, because they wouldn't be controllable if they believed that they were great and wonderful beings. If they can be led to believe that they are only small cogs in a big wheel, they can be more easily managed. That's roughly the kind of thought that has been encouraged by society. People accept it because they are convinced by it. Moreover, they feel that they haven't got the power to do anything else, and they just go on with it. That doesn't mean that we should all become conceited and say, "I'm the greatest." The point I am making is that we do not know what our true being is — we are clouding it up with all this confusion. We cannot really settle the question of our true being. We may be much greater than we think, potentially. In fact, if we aren't, I don't see much chance for the survival of the human species.

ME: Yes, we are living in a kind of psychological dust storm that is obscuring the possibility of any real perception.

DB: We can't see what we really are, and as I said before, we have to question the whole thing. Insofar as we are able to question it, this "dust storm" dies down. We don't know if any of what they say about us is true; maybe we're being sold a bill of goods.

ME: This kind of incoherent and confused thought, is that present at the level at which thought generally works in its rather unsubtle way?

DB: Intelligence could dissolve that. Such thought comes from memory; it's on the disk. Suppose you had a computer that had all sorts of crazy things on it. There have actually been such cases with all these computer viruses that instruct the computer to spread the same instructions to other computers. In this way, a vast number of computers may eventually be so occupied with the virus that they would not respond to the programmer, and necessary programs may even be destroyed. You could say that this is a good analogy to what happens in the mind. This "virus" has communicated itself throughout our society, and the brain is thoroughly occupied with it as well as disrupted in its function. As a result, intelligence, which we would compare to the programmer, is no longer able properly to affect the brain.

Could there be some way of getting that sort of thing off the "disk"? We are actually overwhelmed by this "disk," which fills our brains with all sorts of meaningless misinformation. And the more television, newspapers, and things of this nature we have, the more rapidly the virus spreads. So we've got to question what we're doing and slow it down. Indeed, as we said earlier, when we question it, it does slow down. Perhaps then we can pay attention, and intelligence may be able to operate, making it clear that we are really caught up in something crazy that has no meaning whatsoever.

ME: About this process of questioning, of perception, of looking directly without memory and seeing how memory comes in, you're suggesting that if this process is sustained, it can begin to bring us to perceive how illusion is created.

DB: We're not saying that we're going to do it entirely without memory, without thought; that's impossible. But memory has to come to order, and it cannot order itself. As said earlier, a more subtle and more creative intelligence is needed that can order memory. It's got to understand and see what memory is, so that it can bring it to order.

ME: Can you explain what you mean when you use the word *creative?*

DB: It can't really be defined, because to be creative has no specifiable limits. But we can discuss what it means to be uncreative. There are three things: you can be mechanically stuck in repeating certain patterns; you can be destructive rather than creative; and you can be mediocre rather than creative. The word *mediocre* has an interesting root: in Latin it means halfway up the mountain. You can imagine people climbing up the mountain having strong intentions and giving a high value to their goal of climbing the peak. But halfway up, some begin to feel that being comfortable and safe and secure has a still higher value, and so they stop. However, those who passionately want to get to the top keep going. Evidently, a similar passion is needed for creativity, and without this, one will be caught up in mediocrity. Moreover, it is also clear that creativity is not compatible with being caught up in mechanical patterns, nor with reacting to frustration with destructive rage, hate, and violence. And as I have already said, rewards and punishments also tend to damp down the urge toward creativity.

Creativity is, in my view, a natural potential, but it is largely blocked by the way in which civilization has developed. We have been suggesting that in some sense people in early times were living a more fundamentally creative life than we do now. Of course, they created not only tools and useful objects but also ornamental and religious objects. What was creative, however, was that they were not following a mechanical routine, that it was for them in some sense always new. There is no way to make a mechanical routine when you live in nature like that. Also, they had no reason to be as destructive as we are (maybe occasionally so). The third point was they could put in their whole energy and not be mediocre in what they were doing. We don't know if it was that ideal, but just for the sake of discussion, let's imagine such a state. They may have been a lot closer to that state than we are, though, of course, we are not saying that their lives were perfect.

ME: It would mean the intelligent use of the mechanical operation of thought but not being a slave to it or being just mechanically repetitive. Perhaps one would be using the mechanical to express something creative.

It seems to me that one of the things that blocks creativity in the way we live are these very powerful assumptions that we've all made, many of which we're not aware of having. Clearly, we need to have assumptions; the difficulty is that we don't have assumptions that perceive their own limits.

DB: Yes, I think that is an important point. The mind has to be free and ready to explore these assumptions, not fixed to them. In most of the history of humanity there has been fixing of assumptions, especially those that people are identified with. The fixing of assumptions is usually a kind of conditioned reflex in which one feels these assumptions to be fixed truths. You don't know you're doing it. You implicitly deny that they are assumptions, and instead treat them as truths. Already a "magical" trick of exchanging an assumption for a truth has taken place; thus you are caught up in the creation of illusion.

ME: Doesn't this happen socially and collectively as much as it does with individuals?

DB: Yes. Society takes certain assumptions as truths because it supposes that they are necessary for its stability. Such social assumptions therefore cannot be questioned — very often you can't even mention them, much less question them. There's a tremendous pressure to stop us looking at these assumptions, or if we do look at them, to defend them in a very violent way. The defense of social assumptions can lead to the ultimate violence, to war, to murder, and to oppression, along with the most extreme self-deception and general decay of society and of the individuals who make it up. People feel very uneasy about questioning the basic assumptions of their society.

ME: It's often hard to know what our basic assumptions are, whether these be individual or collective, for we are not generally aware of them. For example, I find great difficulty with Christianity. Is this the result of an assumption?

DB: I think so. Your attitude to Christianity clearly must be strongly affected by your assumptions; perhaps something about Christianity makes you suppose that it is bad. Moreover, Christians may have similar assumptions about atheists, as Moslems may have about adherents of other religions. There may be an assumption that my religion or my lack of religion is right and that yours is wrong. Such assumptions are shared by many people, as a rule, and as you just said, they are very hard to question or, indeed, to be conscious of. As we've been saying, you simply react with a conditioning reflex according to your assumptions. And in this way, you are caught up in all sorts of illusions about other people and about yourself.

People similarly react to defend assumptions and thus create illusions about the nature of the economic system or the social system. Indeed, if you question the economic system or the social system, people may then tend to feel that you are threatening everything, because they are afraid that everything may fall apart. Therefore there is a very powerful defense of such assumptions, often by means that are self-deceptive and distorted. We've seen this in many cases in modern history, when people have defended their social and economic assumptions by false and violent means.

Then there are a great many people who want to change society and don't accept all the assumptions. But they often have their own assumptions. When they take power, they defend their assumptions in the same way (if not worse). And this leads, of course, to a different set of illusions.

ME: But suppose that you have begun to see the futility of this sort of defense of assumptions against evidence that they may be false. What is involved in bringing this process to an end?

DB: As I've already said, it is essential to become aware of our assumptions, especially of those that we tend to defend in this way. In doing this, we can question not only these particular assumptions but the whole state of mind that is disposed to such a defense. The more we do this, and the deeper we go into it, the more we get some sort of feeling for it. In principle, we have to be ready, in this way, to explore the whole idea of assumptions.

In such an exploration, it is important to be aware of the relationship between thoughts and feelings. This sort of awareness can be facilitated in the way suggested in chapter 2, by using words to call up emotional responses so as to make their connection to the intellect stand out, as it were, in relief. In doing this, one can see that anger, for example, is being sustained by certain assumptions, such as that the failure of someone who I thought was my friend to support my self-esteem is unforgivable. Similar assumptions may be discovered underlying fear — that certain anticipated possibilities would be beyond my capacity to deal with them — and jealousy — that it is intolerable that someone else is in what was always my place. To find and use the words that express such assumptions explicitly and thus intensify the corresponding emotions can be very helpful in making it evident how mechanical the whole process is. Indeed, if one is sufficiently serious, one can go even further with this line of exploration by finding and using a set of words that begins to express the kinds of assumptions that lie behind the overall process of self-deception and creation of illusion; for example, I will not be able to manage to organize myself if I can't think certain thoughts that seem to support my sense of self-esteem, even if these thoughts are false.

In doing this sort of thing, we must, however, keep in mind that we need assumptions, and that there is no point in trying to get rid of assumptions as a whole. Indeed, the entire culture contains a basic set of shared assumptions. As long as these can in principle be questioned, and are capable of being negotiated, we can get somewhere. However, if they cannot be questioned and are nonnegotiable, then we can get nowhere, and we will continue to be caught up in illusion. But in fact the basic assumptions of societies are often not capable of being questioned or negotiated. Thus, in Geneva there has not yet been any really serious discussion, because people can talk only about secondary sorts of questions that they can allow themselves to negotiate. The fundamental assumptions that are behind the trouble are not negotiable, at least at present. People identify with such assumptions, which are generally tacit and even hidden. Also, as I've said, they are very frightened that if they let such assumptions go, everything would collapse. Somehow we've got to hold fast in the face of such fears and keep on observing. If we do, we'll see that everything won't collapse just because we are questioning assumptions. It doesn't have to anyway. If we act like fools, then we may indeed produce a disaster. But we needn't be that foolish. We have to question these assumptions seriously, simply because we want to see what is true and because we know that it is no use not being grounded in truth.

ME: I wonder if there is anything more to religion or politics, for example, than a set of assumptions.

DB: At present, there's not a great deal more. There isn't a lot of clarity and honesty in today's society, nor has there been for a long time.

Of course, many people have tried to organize a good society and have dedicated themselves to this. Einstein said that one of the main meanings in life was to devote oneself to the betterment of society; I myself felt that way for a large part of my life, and I know many other people who have. And it seems reasonable at first. But society as we know it has no real foundation. You can't build anything on its basis, because it's all grounded in this thought process that is set to create illusion. Therefore, what you think you see is very often not there, and you can't build on what is not there. So none of the institutions of society as it actually is are the way we think they are, and none of them provides the kind of security or stability that is needed.

ME: As an example of what you are saying, we see today that in trying to satisfy people's material needs capitalist society causes catastrophic environmental destruction, and that it is not really set up to change in the way that is needed.

DB: Environmental destruction in Eastern Europe is even worse, and one can hardly say that their bureaucracies are able to function any better to end this destruction.

However, one very important positive point in all this is that attention has now been brought to these questions throughout the world. Previously, few would even listen to any attempt to discuss this sort of issue.

It is gradually becoming more and more clear that none of these old systems can really work in a sustainable way. And we can now see that the reason is that they are all based on the kind of self-deceptive thought that contains the implicit necessity to defend itself against evidence that it is not correct. Socialism is one such a system of thought; capitalism is another.

ME: Might there be a political movement that wouldn't be based on this sort of thought that creates illusion?

DB: I don't know that we can start by thinking about political movements. People may share certain ideas about what to do, but the basic point would be to look at the state of mind that doesn't hold rigidly to ideas and to discuss how that would work socially. What is needed is a society in which assumptions are not defended against evidence of falseness. You could say that you will defend assumptions up to a point, saying, for example, "I believe these are true; I'll give you my arguments." But they are not nonnegotiable, they do not resist evidence of their falseness. In other words, we are really aimed at getting at the truth and do not want to defend our basic assumptions just because we are identified with them. However, this would evidently be a very uncommon way of talking, though it's clearly the only sensible way. How can the human race survive if it doesn't do that?

ME: One of the problems is that when you get two people sitting down on opposite sides of the table, even if they feel a questioning of the truth of the values that they hold, in the debate they'll support their own assumptions more and more strongly as they go on in the face of opposition.

DB: In this case, you feel that your basic assumptions are a part of you; you're not paying attention to the thought process. It's building up from memory, and you don't notice it.

We have a society, and we have a culture — these are really two aspects of the same thing. The society is the link of relationships, of institutions, of stable structures set up to work together. Culture is the shared meaning behind it; without the culture the society couldn't exist.

We can take as an example a government, which obviously is an institution necessary for a modern society. The government wouldn't exist without a common shared meaning, which includes a set of assumptions about what the government should be doing. Obviously in different countries they have different assumptions, and these may clash. Even within the same country people generally have different opinions about what these assumptions should be. This may lead to political divisions, eventually to civil war.

If we can have a way of negotiating such questions, obviously that is right. Democracy was an attempt to establish a way of negotiating in this manner. But if we don't understand how thought works, democracy won't be very successful in bringing about these negotiations, for we will still defend our thoughts, even when they are false. If two political parties try to negotiate, and each is disposed to defend false thoughts at all costs, it doesn't mean anything. If one wins, it will bring about the victory of false thoughts; therefore, it will do something wrong. This would not be a way of arriving at a coherent and correct approach. In order to have a true democracy, we have to have a different kind of thought process.

Let us go into some of our nonnegotiable assumptions. For example, there are assumptions behind nationalism, and you're generally not allowed to question them. If you do question them, people will either ignore you or they will defend their assumptions falsely. Eventually

168

they'll attack you and say that you are putting the whole country in danger. This will lead them to engage in some violent defense of their assumptions. You can't discuss this issue intelligently, especially in times of crisis. The operation of intelligence is thus prevented by the assumptions behind nationalism and religious fanaticism and political ideology. The brain is affected by these assumptions, so that it cannot allow intelligence to operate and has to block everything. Indeed, you could say that literally something goes wrong with the brain in these cases that we have been discussing. The general point here is that the kind of culture we have can affect each individual brain profoundly.

ME: It seems that a kind of subtle brain damage has taken place in us.

DB: Yes, I believe so. Some people who work on the brain have tried to prove that there is subtle brain damage that can be induced in animals, and under certain conditions you can see that it could easily happen in human beings, though it needn't be irreversible (whereas with serious brain damage, for example, it often is).

I want to emphasize again that we need a culture that doesn't act in a way that may damage the brain by defending its basic assumptions against evidence that they are false. As I've already said, we do, of course, share assumptions, but we have also to discuss our assumptions freely without such a defense and to be ready to change them if necessary. That kind of culture doesn't exist at present, and probably never has existed. The ancient Greeks allowed some questioning, and they had their amphitheaters where at least all free men who were citizens could come and say anything, in principle. But in fact they couldn't always say anything they wanted to; they got rid of Socrates because he said things that they didn't like to hear. As unusual as they were, they were still caught up in it. But other nations at that time didn't come anywhere near the ancient Greeks in their freedom.

ME: We now have Hyde Park Corner in England! At the present time what people generally say with the freedom we've got is simply to insist that their assumptions are right and other assumptions are wrong. We may have the mechanism for a free exchange, but we are unable actually to use the freedom in a creative way.

DB: There are two words that are interesting in this context: *convince* and *persuade. Convince* means to win, basically by defeating the arguments of the other person. *Persuade* is based on the same root as *suave* and *sweet*. In other words, you either win by sweet talk or by strong talk. But both are unintelligent. Indeed, it is a recipe for disaster to stick only to persuasion and conviction. But if you removed persuasion and conviction from our current politics, what would be left?

ME: I like the analogy you made recently of a discussion being like a game of Ping-Pong in which there was not a winner or a loser.

DB: The word *discussion* has some connotations that may not be quite right here. The root of the word is the same as *percussion* and *concussion* — it does suggest this Ping-Pong ball going back and forth, but usually people play to win. Very rarely do they play just for the game.

In politics we've got to get to a situation in which everybody wins in each move — a win-win game, rather than a win-lose game. We have the wrong game at present. We've got to have a certain freedom to do that, a spirit of inquiry, free from fear. People are frightened; they feel they've got to win, if only for their own self-esteem. If you lose, you feel that your self-esteem is wounded, therefore you identify with winning. If we start questioning this, we have some hope of moving toward something better. We will begin to slow down this process of thought; the disks won't operate so rapidly and produce such powerful memory-based feelings.

ME: And perhaps we will ask questions about the nature of our own assumptions?

DB: We must ask questions about ourselves and about everything else, partly because that's the only right way to do it. We may see a stronger reason for doing this by noting that the present situation looks intolerable in the long run and that we had therefore better do something of this nature. But even if things were going right, we still would have to be constantly questioning, because we can't afford just to let thought run away with itself, to trap us in one illusion after another. We have to keep on questioning ourselves, other people, our relationships, our government, our culture, and the various subcultures. Every culture is broken into subcultures, so we need to have these subcultures meeting and negotiating their differences. But if they can't question their own basic assumptions, that will not be possible.

170

ME: People might regard what you've just said as merely a call for tolerance.

DB: Tolerance means that you are going to agree to let the other person be but you're not taking him or her very seriously. Even then, you may get so annoyed that you stop tolerating. There have been long periods of religious tolerance that later turned to oppression.

ME: Yes. Tolerance is evidently not a very creative relationship. It's merely putting up with, rather than having a dialogue.

DB: You don't really take other people's views seriously. You say, I don't mind if they have them, but I'm not going to listen. But that means that we are not going to be able to get together in a culture in which we share our meanings. In a good culture we have to share our meanings and participate together in making a common meaning that is coherent and free of illusion. This is a dynamic process; there is no permanent common meaning of this nature. It's got to be remade all the time. We shall go into this process in some detail in chapter 5, where we talk about it in terms of dialogue.

But the kind of sharing of meaning just described is prevented because we are attached to the present approach and we get frightened when it is questioned. We also feel that the present approach rewards us in certain ways, and we don't want to give that up. So there are many ways in which we find it difficult to think about changing this, even though we are often very unhappy about it. There's that famous saying — the devil that you know is not as bad as the devil that you don't know. But that's an assumption! This devil that we know is pretty bad, because we can see that in a few hundred years at most it's very likely to end our civilization, if not our very existence as a species. Thus we may think that the danger of nuclear war has now receded, but I think it is now clear that it could still come back. People are not really in control of that. As for the environmental problems, we have hardly touched them yet. And the growth of technology will almost certainly create new problems. So, as has already been suggested in part I, it's very hard to imagine that we can go on for as much as a thousand years at this rate; even a hundred years looks optimistic. We can't tolerate this, unless people simply ignore the danger. It is as if they were saying that they don't want to think of what is going to happen to their grandchildren, although they give the appearance of caring for them.

ME: This chapter has been concerned with illusion and reality. One of our main difficulties is that we have the illusion that the present political systems are going to work. On the face of it, there do indeed seem to be various institutions that might solve pollution problems, as well as environmental and social problems, and that might somehow enable nations to get together so that peace will break out all over the world. But that is part of the illusion of thought. We have to be very wary of this, because, as has been made clear, thought simply isn't going to be enough in the long run.

DB: I think we have made it clear that in the long run it is most unlikely that this sort of thing will work. There are going to be ups and downs, but, as pointed out in chapter 2, in history every time there has been an improvement there has been a reaction that largely wiped it out, or went in some other direction. Or else, it turned out that there was another very serious problem that hadn't been anticipated. This overall process of thought that is self-deceptive and defends itself against evidence of its falseness will just go on indefinitely creating more and more problems.

ME: Of course, there are always going to be unexpected problems. That's not the main point. The main point is that thought resists evidence that it is wrong, and thus creates illusions, which constantly lead to new and more complex problems, which are insoluble when treated on an illusory basis.

DB: I think we've made it clear that we are not going to be able to deal with this without changing the nature of thought in some fundamental way. The essential point is the understanding of the nature of thought and the perception of how thought works so that thought can be aware of what it is doing. The more insight into this question, the better.

One can, as suggested by Bruce Wiltshire, obtain a useful insight into those questions by comparing the content of consciousness to a show produced by actors (see *Role Playing and Identity* [Bloomington: Indiana Univ. Press, 1982]). Within consciousness is a display or a show of the meaning of each perception and each thought. The display of the meaning of a thought may take the form of an image, or of a feeling, or of a fantasy, or it may just be a set of words.

One can carry the analogy between consciousness and an actor's show quite far. Thus, in the actor's show a person may represent a certain character by playing a role. There are also all sorts of props, which make the show seem more real. Props are real things whose meaning lies not in what they actually are but in something else that supports the show.

It is evident that thoughts too can lead us to play roles and thus to re-present ourselves in a false way, especially those thoughts that deceptively build up our self-esteem: I am a great, wonderful person who is capable of running everything, and everybody sees that this is so. Such roles are also supported by props. Thus, it is clear from this example that other people can serve as props. Memory-based emotions, as well as mental images, can also do this. Even neurochemicals can act as props. They may, of course, be real signals, as when you are faced with a dangerous animal, for example. But if you are faced with failure of people to accept your role, on which is based your self-esteem, then the neurochemicals can be used to enable you to respond in a way that would make your role more credible to others. Thus, by a convincing emotional display, a person in authority may manage, in spite of poor actual performance, to give a show of someone who is in command of the situation, while the people around him or her are thus led to give a show implying that this is so. Of course, all this is illusion, but clearly something real is going on that creates and sustains such illusion.

In an actor's show, you know that it *is* a show and not to be taken literally, so ultimately you are not caught up in illusion. However, the show that goes on in "real life" is generally taken literally, as what is actually the case, and the props help to conceal that it is a show. As long as it is concealed that it is a show, you can, for example, get much greater pleasure from the neurochemicals. If somebody tells you how wonderful you are, it produces nice neurochemicals, and you get pleasure, but if you see that this is only a show that person is putting on, the neurochemicals won't work nearly so effectively. You've got to believe it if it is to work. To believe it, you must, of course, be able to conceal from yourself that it is a show.

This sort of concealment is evidently a key part of the self-deceptive defense of what is false that we have been discussing throughout. As was explained in chapter 2, this process probably started very early, but it built up as civilization went on and more and more thought was used. By now, it has built up so far as to give rise to all the crises that we have been discussing, but in such a way that it is "hidden" that this thought is actually their source. What hides this is evidently just the process that I have been describing, in which the show of consciousness contains a tendency to conceal the fact that it is a show and even to conceal that such concealment is taking place. In this general process of concealment, the role of thought in bringing this about is what is most hidden.

ME: If consciousness is a show, one may ask, Who is watching the show?

DB: This is one of the questions about which we are the most confused. The traditional assumption of most cultures has been that somewhere deep inside one's whole being, there is a separate "self" who is "doing the watching." This assumption is on the "disks" of memory, and therefore, it operates so rapidly and "realistically" that it creates what appears to be an actual experience of a separate self. But I suggest that it is an illusion that there is such a separate entity who responds to all that happens. Rather, the whole system is "watching" the show, to know what to do. All the neurochemicals, the emotions, the intellect, and so on are taking their cues from the show and are thus in a sense "watching" it (without the intermediation of this assumed separate entity). In this process, one's whole being is profoundly affected by the show.

But as we have seen, the show is full of false content, not only about the world in general, but also about itself. This is very close to the source of the overall process of creating illusion. Such illusion contains a representation of society, of yourself, of your friends, family, and so on. It is all very "realistic." But what seems to be the most important as well as the most real is the sense that consciousness as a whole is clearly divided into two distinct parts. One of these consists of the general content that is being observed; the other consists of a separate "self" that is observing the first part. But it follows from what I have said that this is a fictitious division, which constitutes a fundamental kind of fragmentation. This fragmentation introduces a false split in what may be called the very heart of one's being. Because this division appears to be so important, everything else is divided up in such a way as to support it and to give it the appearance of being secure. You may know abstractly that it isn't actually secure, but this does not greatly affect the feeling and the sense of reality of this whole experience.

It is clear from all this that the process of creating illusion is as much collective as it is individual, and that everyone shares in helping to give these illusions a sense of reality. To be free of this whole process of creating illusion, we have to go on with the sort of inquiry and work that we have been discussing earlier, but collectively as well as individually. In the next chapter we shall discuss how to approach this question collectively through dialogue.

Chapter 5

DIALOGUE AND COLLECTIVE THOUGHT

MARK
EDWARDS:
We have been exploring the view that the only fundamental approach to the problems that we face is through the participation of people around the world prepared to give sustained attention to the process of thought. You said at the end of the last chapter that this had to be done not only individually but also collectively. I think that it would be interesting at this point to see how a group of people might work together to this end.

DAVID
BOHM:
Yes. I think that this is a very important aspect of our inquiry, and I want to suggest that what we need is an extension of what is generally meant by the notion of dialogue. Now as I said earlier, the derivation of a word often suggests a deeper meaning. The word *dialogue* has a Greek root, *dia* plus *logos*. Now *logos* means "the word," but presumably not just the word here but also the meaning. And *dia* means "through," not "two." This suggests that the meaning is passing through or flowing between the participants. We can distinguish this from the usual sort of conversation or discussion. As I said in chapter 4, the word *discussion* has the same root as *percussion* and *concussion*. It suggests a Ping-Pong game in which we are passing the ball back and forth between us, and the purpose is to win.

In a discussion, you might occasionally accept part of another person's view in order to strengthen your own. You might say, I agree with this and disagree with that, but fundamentally you want your view to prevail.

Now I think that dialogue has in it the connotation or flavor of something very different. We are not trying to win in a dialogue. As suggested in chapter 4, it is an activity in which we all win if we're doing it right. We're not against each other in any real sense. From this point of view, you could say that a lot of what's called dialogue is not really dialogue but is more like a discussion, for in a discussion people generally want to make points, but in any case they usually discuss fairly superficial issues. And as we said about the so-called dialogues in the United Nations, the real issues are seldom discussed. In a true dialogue, however, we have to be open to talking about the deeper issues, rather than just staying on the surface of things.

It may be surmised that something like dialogue has been the condition of the human race for perhaps 99 percent of its existence, while people lived in small hunter-gatherer groups. I remember reading a long time ago an article by an anthropologist that struck me very deeply. He said that he went into a certain North American Indian group that was of a hunter-gatherer type. We must distinguish this from agricultural groups and more highly organized tribes with a lot of people in them, where what he said might not apply. He said that they sat around in a circle at night or at any time and talked and talked. There was no visible center and no visible authority. They made no decisions, but they just stopped when they felt they had done enough talking. Yet apparently they all knew what to do, as they understood each other so well in the simple life of the group. As soon as I read that, it seemed to me that this would be the right way to live.

But this doesn't seem to be possible, as we've said in earlier chapters, once we organize bigger social units in which to do agriculture or industry. In these units you get a breakdown of this spirit. In that small unit they didn't need police to enforce things; they didn't need jails to punish people; they didn't need rewards to get them to gather food and so on. We've discussed all this before. Of course, going back to the early Stone Age is somewhat speculative, so I don't want to make too much of a point of it; I am just saying that it is very interesting that something like this seems to have been almost certainly the general way of human life for most of our existence as a species.

ME: Rather than to try to return to this sort of life, might we not learn by looking at such examples and go from there in a creative spirit to bring what is essential in the dialogue to our more modern, complex society?

DB: In answer, I am going to discuss here some ideas that were originally suggested to me by Dr. Patrick de Mare, who works in London as a psychiatrist. (See *Koinonia* [London: Karnac, 1990].) He has developed his ideas starting from small therapeutic groups but has extended them to larger groups of about twenty to forty people sitting in a circle. This arrangement enables each person to be directly related to all the others without a center of authority. There is no leader as such, but there is a facilitator, who initially helps guide the proceedings in as unobtrusive a way as possible and aims eventually to make his or her function unnecessary.

The aim of such groups is not psychotherapy but something much broader. De Mare likes to call it sociotherapy rather than psychotherapy. He feels that the main sickness is in society and that this approach could help to change basic social relationships, in a way that begins with these large groups but ultimately could spread to society as a whole.

One of the key points about such a group is that it is a kind of microcosm of the general society and culture. It may therefore develop all the typical problems of a society at large, including polarization, pressure toward conformity, fear of being judged inadequate by one's "tribe," and so on. Moreover, being in this sort of group tends to lead people to engage in playing their habitual roles (and this is hardly surprising, because basically roles take their meanings only in a collective context). Some will play an assertive and even dominant role to show what great people they are; others will fall into their habitual roles of inferiority because they are terrified of showing themselves up as fools before so many people. It is important for the group as a whole to face various unpleasant difficulties of this sort and in this way to begin to learn how the process of collective thought is actually working, rather than to evade such issues in order to feel more comfortable.

Many of the problems encountered by people in large groups are rather similar to those they meet as individuals or in smaller groups. But usually, in a large group, the problems are considerably intensified by factors of the kind that I have just pointed out. Thus, one will find that people tend to defend their opinions in an even more rigid and nonnegotiable way than they would do when only a few people are present. This is often because they feel a need to win an argument about their opinions in order not to lose face in front of so many people, and this need takes priority over that of arriving at the truth about what they are discussing.

ME: But just what *is* an opinion, that it should be so important to defend it rigidly and nonnegotiably, even though it may be false?

DB: An opinion is basically a supposition or an assumption, isn't it? Buy why do opinions so often give rise to such irrational attempts to defend them? This is evidently because people identify with their opinions, so that they are defending them as if they were defending themselves. They do this in various ways, for example, by rationalizing their positions with arguments that are made to appear to be reasonable but that can be seen actually to be irrational when looked at more closely. There are many other ways of falsely defending opinions against evidence of their incorrectness. To do this in any way whatsoever makes true dialogue impossible.

Much of the talk that people now have in large groups is initially of this defensive nature. Moreover, for the reasons that I have given, some people feel especially impelled to assert themselves and defend themselves in these large groups. And if they feel that they can't do this, they remain silent. Yet if we don't manage to have groups of this size or larger working together in a more rational and effective way than this, how are we ever going to organize society?

ME: This difficulty is not just in thought. Evidently, especially in a large group, very powerful emotions are aroused in the defense of opinions. Indeed, these emotions compel people to hold to their opinions even when they have indications that these may be wrong. How can the group handle such powerful responses? It could so easily fall into chaos, or, as you have indeed already suggested, into a nonnegotiable confrontation between polarized subgroups (a miniature version of the UN).

DB: What is going on in this case is rather similar to the process that I described in the previous chapter, in connection with anger in the individual. The intellect gives false reasons why certain opinions must be defended, while the emotions create pressure against a proper examination of these reasons. It is therefore not just an intellectual problem; nor is it just an emotional problem. It is both together inseparably. As

180

a typical example, there may be the thought which I have already mentioned, that I've got to defend my opinions or I will look like a fool. Emotionally, I feel that I couldn't bear that, so I cannot possibly change my opinion, even if I suspect that it is wrong. So we end up defending opinions against evidence that they may be false, which is a basically destructive kind of behavior.

ME: Given that we don't ordinarily see that this is happening, what can we do to bring it out?

DB: Yes, it is all more or less concealed. That's part of the self-deception and illusion that we're talking about in the previous chapter, but it is now coming up in a collective setting. And what can we do, that is the question? Let us not treat it as a problem, because as we said earlier, we do not clearly see the end that we might wish to achieve. This too has to be discovered as we go along.

The proposal is that dialogue will be a key way to reveal what is actually happening in human relationships in groups of the kind that we are talking about. The first suggestion is that in doing this, it will be important for us to *suspend* our opinions, rather than either to defend them or to suppress them or to avoid expressing them in order to try to prevent conflict. To suspend something is, as it were, to keep it "hanging in front of you," constantly accessible to questioning and observation. You cannot do this if you are defending an opinion, because to defend it, you must accept the assumptions behind it, rather than question them. But if you suppress your opinions or avoid expressing them, you also cannot question or observe them. Nor is it of any use to say that you shouldn't be having certain opinions. If you do this, you may, of course, immediately feel that you don't have them. You would then say, "I am not defending my opinions." You are thus denying that you are defending your opinions, and you even feel that you are not doing it. But other people still see you as doing it. To become unaware of defending your opinions will make it impossible to question them or to observe their operation. All this means that to feel free to express your opinions, regardless of how foolish or wrong they may seem to be to others, is a key requirement for dialogue.

ME: Yes. Even people who might not actually voice an opinion could still react in the irrational way that has just been described and nevertheless feel they were not defending their opinions, when in fact they were actually doing so in their own "internal dialogue." But, as you say, they do not feel free to express their opinions, and until they do, the process of dialogue is impeded.

DB: That's what often happens. Similarly, people might be very polite to each other and not want to stir up a discussion that could cause trouble, so that they would skirt every difficult issue.

ME: Yet, if they do allow such opinions to be expressed freely, the whole atmosphere could, as we have already suggested, become highly charged emotionally.

DB: If the opinions are important to the people, there will be such an emotional charge. If they don't politely avoid the issue, then the charge will sooner or later come up. In a certain group that I attended, there were people with conservative opinions and people with radical opinions. They didn't want to fight each other, and for a long time they did not discuss politics at all and instead found something else they could talk about together without conflict. But in the long run, it is clear that if they kept on meeting, this would sooner or later break down.

The next important point is that if people are to be able to learn to face this sort of emotional charge, they will have to sustain the dialogue and meet regularly for a long time. Suppose, for example, that they met once a week or perhaps once in two weeks and kept this up for a year or two. Eventually people with conflicting opinions or assumptions, such as these conservatives and radicals that I have just been talking about, would be very likely to say something to each other that would make the group highly excited and perhaps explosive. Something similar could happen as the members of the group began to react to one another's various roles and false defenses of their self-esteem. The crucial point is then whether the group can stay with this and see what is actually happening, rather than either letting the reactions run away into nonnegotiable conflict or else falling back into avoiding such difficult issues.

As pointed out by de Mare, however, the purpose of doing this is not primarily therapy for the individuals concerned; rather, it is to end the collective impediments to free communication within the group. To make this possible, I think that it is important to go fairly thoroughly into the meaning of dialogue beforehand, so that people will realize why they are engaging in dialogue and why it is important. If they really see this, they will stay with the process in the way that I just suggested, even when they are confused and emotionally disturbed by it. Also, others in the group who are less committed to particular opinions may come in to defuse the issue a bit without diverting it altogether. In that situation a change can take place. For everybody can see the whole process both publicly and privately. It's the only thing that's going on both outside and inside. Everybody can see what people mean, both by what they say and by the stance of their bodies. And inside you can feel it too, so that you can see that everybody is in much the same boat. Therefore the content of consciousness is in essence basically similar for everybody.

ME: Is it just the content that is similar, or is it the consciousness itself?

DB: At this level, consciousness is inseparable from its content. For example, if the content is anger, isn't consciousness itself pervaded by anger? Of course, we all have our own ways of being angry, but the underlying process is basically similar.

In a way, consciousness is being shared at such a moment. There is indeed a very strong participation in the consciousness of the group, perhaps stronger than it is in more placid moments. An extreme case of such participation would be an outbreak of real hate, engendered by a conflict of opinions that are very dear to the people involved. This can be a very participatory emotion. People who hate each other can be in a very close bond. Now, if people can stay with that, then they are sharing a basically similar consciousness at a very intense level, and therefore in some sense, the usual state of being divided from each other is no longer operative. At this point, a common insight could bring about a fundamental change, in which the hate could be transformed, because it would be seen that the deeper process in common is much more significant than the differences of opinion that led to hate.

I would like to give here a brief story that may perhaps throw some light on this transformation. I once knew a child psychiatrist, who told me about a particularly difficult case of a young girl of about seven years old who wouldn't talk to anybody. They brought her to him, but nothing he did would induce her to talk. Finally, he shouted out in exasperation, "Why won't you talk to me?" She answered, "Because I hate you!" This stopped him for a while, but he thought he must defuse her hate by bringing in the notion of time. So he asked, "How long will you hate me?" The answer was, "I hate you forever." This was really disturbing, but he found a way to bring in time at a new level by asking, "How long will you hate me forever?" At this point, she saw the absurdity of the trap in which she was caught, and she broke out laughing. The absurdity was, of course, that the intended "forever" must change in time. The whole situation was transformed. The energy that had been in the hate now made possible a strong and friendly relationship, while the removal of the absurd assumptions that had been dominating her opened the way for clear thought on how she had been behaving.

In this case, humor is what defused the issue just enough to allow the transformation. In other cases, it could be something else. In general, what is required is a creative response to the actual situation of the moment that transforms the emotional charge into a feeling of impersonal fellowship and awakens true intelligence. Both of these have been prevented by the locking of mental energy into strongly held opinions or assumptions with their intense emotional charges.

In this connection, it is important to note that fellowship means participation that, as has been said in earlier chapters, is both *partaking of* and *taking part in*. Such fellowship may be present even when only two people are involved, but it can become much stronger and more effective in larger groups. In some sense, each member of such a group partakes of the general consciousness, almost as one might do with food, while taking part in contributing to this consciousness. Even those who are not yet talking are in some sense participatory, not only by partaking of what is going on, but by taking part in an inward response.

ME: You are talking about a fundamental change in perception. Are you saying that we are not as separate and individual as we ordinarily feel?

DB: We operate in several modes. Usually our separateness is accentuated; however, in this sort of dialogue there can arise a common feeling in the group, and the sense of separation is not so sharp. This makes it possible for a group of people to think together; that is to say, each person can then take up and continue the thought of another as if it were his or her own. Thus, thinking is being carried out by the whole group, which constitutes a more powerful instrument of intelligence than is in general possible with an individual. However, this must arise naturally and spontaneously — for example, in the act of dissolving the emotional charge — and cannot come from setting a predetermined goal.

It should be emphasized at this point, however, that even in this situation, we are still also functioning as individuals, although we are also partaking of the common consciousness. It is therefore not like a mindless mob, in which the collective consciousness overwhelms the individual. At any moment, each person may still have his or her own opinion, but as opinions are suspended and shared, they are sooner or later included in the consciousness of the group. There is no compulsion to conformity, nor is there any urge to rebel. Rather, freedom goes together with the constant movement toward establishing an ever new and fresh state of harmony in the group.

ME: It is clear that if such a change occurred within an appreciable number of groups, it could be the germ of a profound and very far-reaching change in the general culture and in society. For as we were saying in the previous chapter, culture is shared meaning. Suppose that we were able to share meanings freely without a compulsive urge to impose our own views or to conform to those of others and without distortion and self-deception. Would this not constitute a real revolution in culture and therefore eventually in society?

DB: Yes. One could say that in this case our group would become a nucleus or germ of a true culture; that is, one that is free of the need to defend itself against evidence that its basic assumptions may be incorrect. It could thus be called a microculture — in the sense of being a microcosm of the new kind of general culture that is possible.

ME: This is really an exciting prospect. But how is this different from therapy groups, T-groups, and so on, which are able to attain "highs" in which they report similar feelings of fellowship and shared experience? In spite of the similarity with what we have been saying about dialogue, I feel such groups are not really able to bring about a sustained and radical transformation of culture of the kind that is urgently needed.

DB: This is a subtle question that requires a careful and extended answer. Let me first of all say what dialogue is not. I have already explained how it differs from a debate or a discussion. But it also does not attempt to focus on removing the emotional blocks of any participant, nor is it aimed primarily at solving problems. What is essential to dialogue is, as you have just indicated, that it is an exploration of the shared meanings that constitute our culture. Such an inquiry into this culture can lead to transformations not only in its content, but also in its movement, and in the dynamical process by which it either degenerates into self-deception and incoherence or opens up into honesty and clarity.

As I have indicated earlier, it is a key requirement that the process of dialogue be sustained with more or less the same participants over long periods, which may even be several years. In such a process, both "highs" and "lows" are mere incidents. Because the participants see the meaning and value of dialogue, they will go on with it in spite of frustration and discouragement. They do not try to hold up the "highs" or avoid "lows." Rather, everything that happens is "grist for the mill" and serves as an opportunity for learning how thoughts and feelings weave together, both collectively and individually. The insights that come out of the process will be constantly freeing us from its coherent features.

Of course, to aim at perfect coherence would make no sense. The general situation that would be appropriate is one in which, while we constantly manifest incoherence, we are constantly ready to acknowledge this rather than defend ourselves against being aware of it. And so we are constantly learning through observing incoherence and thus moving toward coherence. In this way, we are creating the new kind of shared meanings or culture that is required. To my knowledge, other sorts of groups that may look similar in certain ways to dialogue groups are not concerned fundamentally with such questions but have more limited interests.

ME: The emphasis on suspending thoughts and feelings is another important feature that is characteristic of dialogue. Can you say more about this?

DB: Suspension of this kind requires, as I've already said, that people feel free to express their opinions and have enough trust in the group so that they will not be afraid, for example, of making fools of themselves. This will come about eventually, but only if the dialogue is sustained.

What is needed especially is that judgments be suspended—judgments of what is true or false, what is real or illusory, what is necessary or contingent, what is right or wrong, what is beautiful or ugly, what is intelligent or stupid, and so on. To a large extent, in our culture these judgments come out of automatic reflexes of thought and therefore have little value. Indeed, they are very often false and destructive and generate fear, hate, and self-deceptive pleasure. Genuine judgments should come out of an act of perception rather than out of a reflex. But this will not be possible unless the reflexes of thought and feeling are suspended. Because the reflexes are so habitual, however, it is very hard to be aware that they are acting. Such awareness requires serious attention. This is possible with the individual. But in a group of twenty to forty people, each can be aware of the reflexes of others, so the power to draw attention to reflexes can greatly increase the strength of the whole group. Bonded by a sense of fellowship, members of the group can make these reflexive judgments evident to all in a context in which there is no sense of isolation brought about by fear. And so transformation is facilitated.

ME: At this point it may perhaps be helpful to go back a bit and inquire more deeply into the ordinary state of collective thought, which is evidently one of the main barriers to a change of this kind.

DB: Yes. Let us then descend from this broad vision of what is possible and consider once again our ordinary level of thought. Most such thought is indeed collective in origin; for example, the thought of space and time, the thought of the body, the thought of the government, the thought of the family, the thought of art and science. And it is language, clearly a collective activity, that formulates and conveys such thought. The most fundamental thoughts are collective. We share these thoughts. And individuals develop their own thoughts mostly out of the common pool. From this, they learn what society is like, what nature is like, and what sort of persons they should be. Thus, they look to other people collectively to support this image of themselves, which is generally the basis of their self-esteem. For example, the main reason a lot of people want to make money is to improve their self-esteem. They think that the money will cause other people to think well of them, and that this will enable them to think well of themselves. So you see the collective thought enters very powerfully into our society, even though this thought may also say that the individual is the only thing that matters. But this latter, too, has been collectively agreed. In other societies, there have been different agreements.

So although each individual makes his or her own contribution, the whole process is nevertheless primarily collective. Occasionally some people may have an original thought, but for the most part we more or less rearrange thoughts and use them in various contexts, adapting them in suitable ways. From time to time, our perceptions will enrich them. But then we're ultimately adding back into the common pool of thought.

But of course we must not overlook the fact that the individual human being as a whole has his or her own peculiar features, even though many of these are chosen out of the collective pool. These include the body of that person, and also the brain and nervous system. Moreover, each person has certain unique potentialities, based not only on special talents and a particular inherited constitution but also on what has been learned from experiences that are, in some ways at least, different from those of anyone else. But then there is something much deeper that really belongs in a much more essential way to the individual. I would say this involves the possibility of a connection with what I would call the cosmic dimension of life.

I think that the life of a human being has three basic dimensions: the individual, the collective, and the cosmic. We have already discussed the first two to some extent. However, since ancient times, people have had a regard for something greater, the whole, the cosmic. Perhaps in early times people felt very close to nature. Under these conditions nature can be felt as something that gives a sense of the whole that goes far beyond the individual or the collective. Then when people went into cities or onto farms, they began to lose this. Religion helped to make up for it.

ME: Also art.

DB: Yes, art too. Art gave some contact with the cosmic even in very early times, but later, art and religion tended to tie together in doing this. Religion is, of course, aimed at the whole in its own way. Science too is dedicated to giving a view of the whole. In more recent times, many people have ceased to believe in the basic ideas of religion. It doesn't function very well at all now for a large number of people, yet science doesn't give such people a really satisfactory contact with the whole.

ME: It's too complex now.

DB: It's too complex and abstract for most people, though maybe a few can appreciate it. Art gave something to people too, but as we said earlier, we can see that artistic movements are also now generally confused.

It all adds up to the fact that people don't seem to know quite what to do. They've lost contact between art, religion, and science and the cosmic.

ME: Yes. And the individual doesn't have this contact either.

DB: There is also the loss of connection to nature, which I think is crucial.

ME: Could dialogue help to bring about harmony among the individual, the collective, and the cosmic?

DB: This is quite possible. But it will be difficult to approach the cosmic in a coherent way before the individual and the collective are cleared up to some extent. Let us therefore begin with the individual and the collective and see where this leads us.

Now, insofar as all the different people have different assumptions that they defend, they will resist and oppose each other. But insofar as each individual is able to hold all the assumptions together in suspension, they will, as we have seen, share a common consciousness. The word *consciousness* is however based on *conscience*, whose root meaning is "knowing it all together." Originally, it seems that it meant what everybody knows all together. But now it usually means what the individual knows all together. In a dialogue, these two meanings cohere and form a subtle higher unity, in which each individual participates in the whole group in the general way that we have already described. This means that through the dialogue, the individual and the collective can come together into a harmonious unity.

ME: Can we bring the cosmic into this?

DB: Yes, but it is still a bit too soon. We have first to look further into the various things that get in the way of the dialogue.

One of these is prejudice, which means that you've made a prejudgment without even looking. Prejudices are practically all collective in origin. For example, color prejudice comes from parents or friends. A prejudice is a form of collective opinion that is defended against evidence of its falseness. All this will come up in the dialogue. We are committed then to looking into it and to sustaining our work with it. Why do we do that? Because we know it is very important, for reasons that have already been discussed.

As we proceed with this dialogue, you will find that from time to time people may feel bored or frustrated. We have had some experience over the past year or two in some groups and have found that they do get bored and frustrated in this way. But that's only to be expected. Ordinarily people have two reasons for getting together. One is that they will do something enjoyable and have fun. The other is that they will do something useful, even if it's not fun. But here, they're not having fun, and they're not seeing any useful purpose. The natural reaction would be to stop, unless they see the importance of going on. When you know something is important, you will go on with it even if it's not fun and even if it's boring and frustrating. But we are saying that the dialogue is of key importance in the long run; if people can keep sight of this, they'll go on with it.

ME: It seems important that there should be people with different backgrounds, because the group should explore what it is to disagree.

DB: As I've said earlier, everybody has taken a different part out of the general public pool. In fact there are always different subcultures, as you're pointing out, that don't agree with each other. It is good to get a certain mixture of people. But if your group is as large as twenty or thirty, even if they have the same general background you'll find important differences arising anyway.

ME: The difficulty is to get started — to find a room and a good mixture of people who can keep going without an imposed purpose. We have very little experience in this kind of thing.

DB: My experience is that there are many ways in which people may come together — because they have read of the idea and want to pursue it, for example. Another way is to organize a meeting of a day or two while people discuss these questions and bring out the importance of dialogue. Once the perception of its necessity is there, then the rest can follow.

The beginning requires some initiative on somebody's part to get it going. But how is it going to keep going? As I've said, it is important not to have a leader in the long run. You see, one of the points of the dialogue is that it should be on the level; that is to say, people have to be able to be honest and straight with each other. They cannot do this if there is an authority or a hierarchy, however subtle and tacit its operation may be.

As I've said, it is important that the facilitator who gets things going should not impose him- or herself on the group and should work toward making that function ultimately unnecessary. (At present, however, the form of talking in groups that is generally accepted is centered on the leader. Everybody addresses questions to the leader, and the leader answers. But that's not what is called for in a dialogue.) Moreover, because we have a circular form, no person is singled out by the geometric arrangement as more important than any other. You try to get as close to that form as you can. For example, you may have to use two concentric circles or more.

But this is not enough to stop the tendency to have a leader, for everybody wants a leader. It's part of our tradition; people feel insecure without a leader. So the point is, as I have already said, to have a facilitator who gets things going and who may make comments in not too obtrusive a way. This sort of situation will probably go on for some time. Indeed, experience shows that when people are suddenly left with a group that has no specified purpose and no leader, they flounder around and feel lost. They are worried and can become rather anxious. But if they can get beyond this, experience shows they start to talk anyway, and it soon starts to work. You just have to get through an uncomfortable period. But you'll do that, because you know it's important.

ME: Wouldn't it be helpful for the facilitator each time to suggest a topic to talk about, just to get going?

DB: It is important not to impose a question on the group. The group generally comes with its own questions that are implicit. If you impose a question, you are liable to have the authoritative situation, with its repression of real feelings.

ME: Right. You would just be trying to control the process of collective thought.

DB: We are, however, starting a new process going. This process leads to impersonal fellowship and eventually to friendship. As we have seen, the action of intelligence made possible in this way really changes the nature of consciousness. We are beginning to share content freely, and so we are thinking together. But otherwise we're thinking separately so that we're not meeting, and there is little point to it. Now if we think together, then maybe we can solve our common problems.

ME: It's not like having a church either—that would be awful. As you have said, it is important that there is no central figure and no hierarchy.

DB: There is no hierarchy. We are all "leveling" with each other. Nor are we worshiping anything. We are just having this common mind, this shared mind that can think together in a new way. Its movement can be free from all the opinions and automatic reflexive judgments and move beyond them. Generally speaking, you will find that these opinions and reflexive judgments are likely to be irrelevant. Especially if you've been defending them, they're almost certainly too limited to be of any use. Therefore the first process is that we just look at them all, and we can take whatever is worthwhile in them and then stop worrying about them. We then go on to something new and creative, a new mind in which we can begin to free thought from its rigid collective conditioning.

This is important, because, as we're saying, most of our thought is really collective. So even if you look at your thought individually you're going to be rather limited in how far you can go. It's important to do this, but it's not enough. We're saying that with the awakening of intelligence, the more subtle mind can also begin to develop in a collective context. As we have been saying, in such a context the subtle mind is not only a shared operation of subtle intelligence but also the feeling of participation and fellowship and friendship. Without that feeling, which underlies the possibility of mutual trust, it's not going to work.

There are many ways of looking at this. You could say that in some way the emotions could be compared to a kind of music and that this music has to be orchestrated. At present we could say that our emotions as induced by ordinary thought are rather like stirring martial music or possibly sentimental love songs, really unsubtle. But in this dialogue there's going to be a very subtle music, and in fact, you could say it's a kind of dance with music. Now that's an interesting point, because people are able to sing together, to dance together, to do all kinds of things together. But they can't talk together. They can't think together. But evidently we have to talk together and think together if we're going to organize society in a meaningful way. I suggest that if we can sustain a real dialogue, we will find in the end that talking and thinking together is very like a kind of improvised singing and dancing together.

ME: I think it's difficult, because, as we've said many times, one can't set this up as a goal. The minute you feel you are moving toward a goal, you know that ordinary thought is in operation. Exploration of thought does not have a precisely definable end in view.

DB: No, we're merely showing the possibilities.

ME: You seem to feel that without this exploration technological civilization is not going to work.

DB: It's not even practical.

ME: No, it's certainly not. We see the evidence of that a hundred times a day, but we continue trying to modify the old systems.

DB: Some people have said that love would make everything right. As the Beatles said, "All you need is love." And Jesus Christ said, "Love one another." And that's true. If love could really flower, it would work. But the fact is, generally speaking, it can't, given the destructive conditioning of our thought.

To give an example, the two greatest physicists of this century, Einstein and Bohr, got to know each other and to work together. Einstein writes on Bohr that when he first saw him he had a feeling of love for him. They began to talk physics, and at a certain point they disagreed. They had two different opinions about the way to go from there. They talked and talked, and they tried very hard to communicate, much harder than most physicists would have done. They were extremely serious in their wish to communicate and talked it over and over again in a calm and rational way. But it always ended with each one asserting his opinion and saying that the other one was wrong. Einstein said finally that Bohr had a tranquilizer philosophy and that he'd just gently rested his head on this as a pillow; Bohr finally said that Einstein had gone against his own revolutionary achievements. They never agreed, and they gradually lost touch with each other.

Finally they were both at Princeton at the Institute for Advanced Study. But still they had never met. A mathematician called Herman Weyl said that was a pity, they ought to meet. So he arranged a party at the Institute and invited Einstein and Bohr and their students. What happened was that Einstein and his students congregated at one end of the room and Bohr and his students at the other, and they never talked. The reason was very simple; they had nothing to talk about. So you see that which began as love turned into indifference. I wouldn't call it hate. It could have been turned into hate with people of lesser caliber.

ME: Perhaps if they could have loved each other in the way Jesus was suggesting they might have been able to suspend their beliefs for long enough to have gone beyond their own ideas.

DB: As you are implying, such an absolute and total love would have to include a clear perception of the necessity of suspending one's own opinions and beliefs sufficiently to enable one to see without defensive reflexes what the other person really means. But in society, at least as we have known it over the past few thousand years, such love has been very rare indeed. And obviously, it makes no sense to try to *impose* it, nor will we get very far simply by enjoining people to have this love when they don't have it. Rather, we are faced with a situation in which love is generally at best imperfect, while very commonly, there is fear, hostility, aggression, and even hate rather than love. All this arises from the mainly collective conditioning, which is equivalent to a set of "programs" on our "disks" that very rapidly and "realistically" spring into action when, for example, we are confronted by a set of basic assumptions that are different from our own. Thus, even in the case of Einstein and Bohr, the original feelings of love and friendship were in this way blocked by fixed and rigid opinions, which prevented listening and eventually led to each rejecting the other.

ME: Yes. I see that it is necessary to have an approach that works with people as they actually are, rather than with some idealized kind of person who is either very rare or else perhaps does not even exist at all. In the case of Einstein and Bohr, for example, how do you suggest that they could have got beyond the impasse in which they were caught?

DB: I feel that they should have had a dialogue along the lines that we have been discussing. Had they been able to do this, they might have come to the suspension of their particular opinions. This would have made possible a new approach that was much more fruitful and creative, an approach that was not limited by Einstein's notions of relativity or by Bohr's notion of the quantum theory. I have some speculative ideas of my own about how they could have done it. It would carry us too far afield to go into it now, but I think it could in principle have been done.

The lesson one learns from this is that love, as we generally know it, is not enough. The crucial point in the present context is that people have to be able to talk together and think together. If they can't do this, whatever love there may originally be will eventually go. That seems clear. Certainly, the more love there is, the better. But even when there is little or none, it is still possible to explore the question of dialogue.

ME: Are you saying that love cannot operate unless opinions and reflexive judgments can be suspended, that this might be necessary for love to flower? If so, such suspension is much more broadly important than we have been saying thus far.

DB: Yes. Consider, for example, the case of married couples who stick to their opinions and judgments completely rigidly—they are simply going to separate. They've got to be able to talk about and acknowledge their differences in a negotiable way, or else they can't stay together.

ME: What is it that suspends the rigid opinions and judgments? Is it intelligence, or insight that sees that opinions and assumptions are too rigid, too narrow, and cannot encompass reality?

DB: It is seen through intelligence and insight that they don't encompass everything and that they're not all that important. The point is that to have this dialogue between us is more important than any opinion or judgment. For example, I may end up with the same opinion as I had before, but we have changed because we have listened to each other's opinions. Even in the case of quarrels between people, the mere fact that the other person will seriously listen to the opinion without even agreeing is generally enough to stop the quarrel. The worst feature of the quarrel is the feeling that the other person is not listening, so the feeling that he or she is at least listening will cool it down, lower the emotional temperature.

ME: We are very inexperienced in all this, so that we tend to fall into the old ways of argument. But when that happens, we can perhaps explore suspension of our opinions and automatic judgments.

DB: Such suspension of opinion is basically similar to what we have discussed in connection with individual thought in chapter 2. There we suggested holding anger at a "midpoint" between letting it run away into conflict and suppressing it or becoming unaware of it. In dialogue, we are doing the same sort of thing collectively, and the thought process behind it is coming out as we talk. It's really an extension to the collective level of what we were discussing in the previous two chapters.

ME: Yes. And one can also see a very interesting possibility — that this attitude of suspending opinions and automatic judgments and looking at how they actually operate in the collective thought process could spread if groups were established in different places. There could then be an interchange of people who could do this between groups as well. And all this could be done without building up a fixed organization.

DB: You don't need an organization. The group itself needn't be permanent. We can always make new ones.

ME: And in fact it will probably be necessary to make new ones from time to time.

DB: If we start with one group it may seem very small. But to compare this with the development of nuclear energy, this started with just disintegrating a few uranium nuclei. One might have said at the time that this is too small to matter. Nevertheless, it was the beginning of a general process that spread. The same could be true, as we have been saying, about the human mind, if we can touch on some feature of this mind that is general for all people. We're saying that it hardly matters who starts this. We're all similar enough in that regard.

ME: Yes, we hope that ultimately it will change institutions and governments. But the first point is to do it, because it has meaning to do it and because it is interesting to do. We are such strangers to our own mind that in some ways, it's like exploring a foreign country.

DB: As an example of this, we see from experience that people find the idea of a group without a defined and specified purpose difficult. We do, however, have a sort of a purpose, which is to explore talking together and thinking together. But beyond that, the purpose need not be defined.

Any further definition of a purpose would include assumptions that could bring in irrelevant restrictions. For example, we might say that we want to talk about objective scientific things and don't want to bring in personalities. But we know that scientific theories are often affected by personal considerations, so that we may have to bring them in if we are to talk and think together without hidden impediments. Therefore we settle on this notion of a group without a purpose that is any more defined than this. Such an approach creates a great deal of insecurity at first, but we have to face that, to get through it.

To say that we need a group of this kind, without a well-defined purpose, is like saying that we need a place, an empty space. We need an empty space that is not occupied by anything in order to let the mind flower, and from there, we can go on to do all sorts of specific things, being infused by the spirit that develops in this empty space. But if we don't have the empty space, we're going to be stopped.

A key point is that intelligence can then make our action free of the conditioning based on memory. In a way, instinct could be thought of as a racial memory. This is evidently very limited. We have then developed thought to deal with more complex situations, but even thought is not very subtle. And we could say that the whole response of memory, including thought, the memory-based feelings, and the instincts, could be put more or less together, and that the intelligence goes beyond all of them. This kind of subtle mind is essential for us to be truly human and that will make possible real civilization and a genuine culture.

Many people, however, have become discouraged or even cynical and have said that we are necessarily governed by instincts. What such people say is that we are basically driven by instincts, such as aggression, and that the ego is trying rather ineffectively to control these instincts.

I think that what we have been talking about here goes beyond such limited notions. There is an infinitely subtle possibility that can be realized by our total being. This is not bound by the instincts, by our history, or by our thought. It is really open and creative. This is a crucial point.

ME: There are people who can see a certain value in the sort of things that we have been talking about but who think that it is still necessary to focus mainly on some practical questions. They don't see how what we are saying connects to the actual crisis that confronts us, and they don't see really how to make the connection.

If we take the environmental crisis as an example, it is clear from what we have been saying thus far that there simply isn't likely to be very much future for civilization unless there is a fundamental change in thought. There is a lot of evidence to support this idea. Nevertheless, many people say that we simply have to attend to the practical problems.

They feel that this notion of dialogue may be very interesting, and that it may perhaps produce valuable results in the long term. But while we talk, the ozone layer is being depleted; the climate is changing; deserts are spreading; cities are deteriorating; the quality of life everywhere seems to be diminishing. In order to be effective, groups of people have given their energy to certain aspects of the environmental crisis — disappearance of tropical rain forests, pollution in the seas, desertification, and so on. This gives a lot of people a sense of meaning, a sense of doing something positive, of getting something done while people like us sit around talking about the process of thought. Some people with energy and concern would see that as fiddling while the world burns.

DB: Yes. Of course, I don't want to suggest that we should give up all attention to the immediate problem. In fact, as has been said in earlier chapters, we need to pay a lot more attention to this than we have so far. But I feel that without attention to the long-range problem, the deeper one, it won't mean very much. I think that if we just deal with one immediate problem after another, then (it has been brought out sufficiently) we are going to keep on creating new problems, as our thought process defends itself against evidence that it may be wrong. This approach cannot work. Now what I am suggesting is that if we have this unoccupied space, whether it be collectively in the dialogue or individually, where we are free to look and to have this kind of more subtle mind that does not defend itself against evidence that it may be mistaken, this will begin to infuse the rest of our activities, both individually and socially.

Therefore, we're going to have to approach it in two ways at once. First, as has also been suggested in an earlier chapter, we must note that the only proper way for dealing with the detailed problems is simultaneously to look at the general problem. This detailed approach by itself could at best buy time. However good you are at it, you're not going to stop this destruction in the long run. You can perhaps slow it down. But second, dealing with detailed problems can also be a means of mobilizing some energy for the whole inquiry into the mind. In addition it can create a new situation, a more peaceful situation, in which we can more easily carry out this inquiry both collectively and individually.

What I am saying is, then: Go ahead with all these particular activities, but you can surely find time for the other one. If we have a dialogue once a week, or once in two weeks, or if you look at yourself, if you find some leisure each day to do so, I think you will find that your other work will go on much better.

We could sum up by saying we've got to look at thought, both individually and collectively, and that in this process we will come upon some more subtle quality of the mind that will begin to awaken and that can spread. This subtle quality will show up collectively in a sense of impersonal fellowship that generates trust and in the intellect as thinking together in a way that is free of the general pressure toward self-deception that we now feel. This can be the germ of a radically new kind of culture.

Chapter 6

ON MEANING

MARK
EDWARDS:
We have drawn attention to the sense of isolation and unhappiness that affect many people in society who are unable to find any real meaning in their lives. We have also suggested that the approach to dialogue given in the previous chapter and the exploration of the process of thought indicated in earlier chapters could produce a more genuine culture in which meaning could be shared freely. Without this sharing of meaning, there does not seem much point to civilization.

DAVID
BOHM:
Yes, I think that it actually could produce a genuine culture. Perhaps it would be best to begin by going into this whole question of meaning. According to the dictionary the word *meaning* has three definitions. One of these is significance, the second is value, and the third is purpose. Significance is clear; the meaning points to something, indicates something. Then, whatever has a high value is what means a lot to me. And if I say that I mean to do it, this signifies that it is my purpose. It's not an accident that significance, value, and purpose are all involved together in *meaning*, for I think that they are intrinsically related. Indeed, nothing will have high value unless it has a lot of significance. And to generate a strong purpose, there must be a high value in what one is doing, so that there has to be significance to generate that purpose. It is clear, then, that meaning is something very fundamental. When you say that life is meaningless, you are really saying that it has no value. Such an observation may have some significance; it may signify, for example,

that what you are doing is rather limited and mechanical. Everything signifies something, so you cannot totally get rid of significance. But a limited, mechanical kind of significance has little or no value to you. It doesn't generate much purpose, and it gives rise to very little energy to do anything. So in this sense people could say that life in this society doesn't have much meaning if their main occupation is a mechanical sort of work and if they are isolated.

ME: Emotionally isolated and suffocated by crowds — at least in our cities!

DB: Isolation is often sensed as loneliness or lack of meaningful relationships with people. But it can reveal itself in more general ways. For example, we are also isolated in the content of our consciousness. Thus, each of us has our own opinion that we defend, so that we don't share a common content. Moreover, a tremendous number of activities of thought are isolating, because we get committed to them and we feel that we have to defend our basic assumptions; we then can't really listen to somebody else, so we cannot be closely related to other people with different basic assumptions.

ME: I think that in the 1960s especially (although it had been going on, as we know from many other accounts, in earlier times) people turned to drugs to find a new and deeper meaning to their lives. LSD became popular for a time because people felt it made them more sensitive and opened their minds to another way of perceiving reality that appeared to have significance. This came into fashion and went out again without changing things very much. People had to go back to doing dull jobs, which actually do not have much meaning.

DB: Yes, well, at present that's the way it generally is. We'd have to consider changing society fundamentally, but we couldn't do that without changing the whole consciousness in the way that we've described. Nevertheless, the more a fundamental kind of significance, value, and purpose are lacking, the more people will seek them in all sorts of ways. Some may try to find them in society itself, or in movements to make society better. When I was younger, people still generally believed that society could be made better. Many movements arose. Some believed in democracy; some in socialism or in communism. As we have seen in previous chapters, most of these have lost their original impetus, and some have petered out. Today there is not nearly as much faith as there used to be that any of these could really solve our social problems. At present, a great deal of this sort of energy is going into environmental movements instead. But as we shall discuss in more detail later, even those are in danger of losing their sense of meaning, if people cannot communicate properly and instead remain isolated from each other.

In such a situation, some people try to find meaning in pleasure, but then that's obviously very limited. It loses its attractiveness if you just go on with it mechanically.

ME: Yes, it becomes boring eventually. But the brain demands meaning, and if there isn't any, it invents it: God, football, or something else.

DB: Even in the Bible they talked of the same thing. As Ecclesiastes said, "Vanity of vanities; all is vanity." It's an old problem; it hasn't just been introduced lately, though, as you say, it seems to have got worse.

We suggested in the last chapter that genuine meaning could be produced and generally sustained only through the action of subtle intelligence. The crude kind of thoughts and feelings that we now generally have will have very little significance and will not give us much sense of value or purpose. People can get very excited about football or something similar, but after all, they can't live on that. So we have a crisis. The crisis of meaning is not only a crisis of culture, it is also a crisis of consciousness, for meaning is at the core of consciousness. Without meaning, what is consciousness? If there were no significance, value, and purpose, would there be consciousness? It would just be a machine.

Many of the people who take drugs hope to come to a deeper meaning in this way, and thus to change consciousness. For a moment it may appear that they do so, but the inadequacy of the meaning leads to addiction, and that creates new problems. Some of the American Indians used to use drugs to change consciousness, but they connected it up with some kind of broad cultural meaning. Indeed, genuine meaning has to be perceived in an even broader context that includes what I have called the cosmic, as well as the collective and the individual.

You can look at our society and our culture and see that it is quite incoherent, and that it has very little meaning. As pointed out earlier, people used to believe that some kind of meaning was there. When I was a child, it was common for an adult to say that we have had a very tough time, but our children are going to have it better. People no longer believe this now.

ME: We now believe the opposite.

DB: It was always an illusion to expect that it was really going to get better through the technological and political methods that were actually adopted. It has become patent and clear now that this was an illusion.

ME: The point is that we need exploration, which, we hope, will lead us to a way of life that has real meaning. In this mechanical world there is very little to explore within the routine laid out by society. You have to begin by looking at things from a point beyond social systems. When we do this, we see very clearly the meaningless state of the present society.

DB: To make up for the emptiness of social relationships, people hope in the family to have a relationship that is not mechanical. And perhaps they get it, up to a point. But then conflicts arise in the family, largely because it's too limited. Meaning depends also on the surroundings. If people lose their jobs, they can't maintain a good family life. And even if they continue to be employed, people are often so dissatisfied that they leave home. You can't find a real solution there either, although as I mentioned earlier, some people say that the main purpose of life is to have a family and raise children. That has indeed been one of the main purposes, and many people still feel this way, but it is becoming less and less viable in an overpopulated world in which more and more families are breaking up. So what *is* the point?

I think that to go further into this we need to explore the question of pleasure, which has always been a very important value in civilization. People have used pleasure partly as a reward to get people to do jobs that did not really interest them deeply. But then, as we explained earlier, people began to seek pleasure just for its own sake, by abstracting the pleasure from the thing that gave pleasure.

ME: Well, another thing that gives pleasure great value is that for a period it obliterates anxiety.

DB: Yes, fill the mind with something pleasurable, and that will get rid of the pain and anxiety for a while. However, we ought to distinguish pleasure from joy or enjoyment. Joy might be a spontaneous part of a whole meaning. You cannot seek joy; if you do, it makes no sense because the very seeking is not compatible with joy. You could say that you can't separate joy from the whole process in which it comes about. But as I've just said, pleasure can be abstracted from the process that produces it. Now the animal can't do this, and therefore for the animal pleasure is a kind of joy. But for us, who can abstract it mechanically, pleasure has become mechanical. (Animals who have long been in contact with humans may be able to respond similarly.)

ME: That's very interesting; I hadn't thought about that before. Could you go into that a bit more?

DB: Well, we give our feelings a name. If you happen to enjoy something but don't abstract it and name it, you won't demand it again.

ME: This is clearly the operation of thought. For example, we were saying at lunch that we enjoyed seeing Woody Allen films. But to do this could well make us want to repeat the experience, perhaps many times, and after a while it would be mechanical rather than enjoyable.

DB: Originally it was not mechanical, because the pleasure was incidental. But then when you abstract pleasure by thought, what you are doing becomes a means to an end, which after some repetition eventually becomes boring. By contrast, joy cannot be an end produced by a means. Joy is a part of the meaning. Eventually you can see there is no point in just constantly seeking pleasure—though there's no point in avoiding it.

Pleasure is always counterbalanced by pain. Wherever you can have pleasure you can have pain; in fact, the nerves are built that way. I saw somewhere an article showing that the pain centers and the pleasure centers are very close, so that when you excite one, you excite the other. Thus, if you stub your toe, you have pain, but when the pain goes away, you get a sense of pleasure. It's very simple. The pleasure came in while you were stubbing your toe, to balance off the pain. As the pain goes away, you get a surplus of pleasure. And similarly, when intense pleasure goes away, you are left with a surplus of pain. The loss of pleasure is therefore painful. So, you see, pleasure and pain are inseparable. The idea that we could separate pleasure and have it always free of pain is a delusion.

In any case, physical pain is necessary too, because it warns us that things are wrong. Without pain we couldn't live. There are people whose pain nerves are so damaged that they can hurt themselves badly and not know it; there would be no point in having pleasure all the time without pain, if as a result you were destroying your body. Pleasure and pain can thus both have significance. In the first instance, their significance is they point out on the animal level that what is pleasant is a good thing to do and that what is painful is not. But then once you can abstract pleasure by means of thought, it no longer means that anymore; it has very little significance.

ME: It seems to me that we would have a true meaning in life, not through pleasure or great achievements or identification with something wonderful, but rather by simply feeling vibrantly alive and by being in our right place.

DB: There's a phrase that Browning used: "God's in his heaven — All's right with the world." That's the sort of meaning we want to get. But we can't say that now. Whatever God is doing, he must have lost interest in us. I think he got bored with us.

ME: It has also been said that one of the main meanings of art is a sense of order — everything in its right place. Then later the word was used to describe the things that a person who led an orderly life produced. Now that we live rather mechanical lives, we think that a sense of order means a rather routine life.

DB: But order is a far more dynamic thing. For example, some mathematicians and scientists are playing with the notion of order in new ways that are reminiscent of Genesis, which begins with the idea that God created order out of chaos, by making the difference between day and night, between land and water, and so on.

ME: And then thought evolved and produced chaos once again!

DB: Yes, well, not being able to grasp this order and work with it, thought has produced chaos essentially because it has not made order in its own process. Thought has generally looked for order in something else, tacitly treating its own process as though it were beyond the requirements of order. But it isn't. We need this more subtle intelligence that is able to keep thought in order. Otherwise, it will start to defend itself against evidence that it may be wrong (in the way we have described in earlier chapters), and this means that there can be no coherent order.

There is an ancient image that is relevant to this whole question, which is that of the rider and the horse. The rider does not order the movement of the horse by power or force, but by very subtle means. In fact, a good rider and a good horse are almost one being. Suppose, then, that we compare intelligence to the rider, and thought to the horse.

This reminds me of the first time I rode a horse. I was in a national park in California, and we wanted to hire a horse. So I got on the horse, and I didn't know quite what to do. The man said, "If you don't think faster than the horse, you'll go where the horse wants to go." This made a deep impression on me; I never forgot it. As we moved along, I found that he was really quite right. With these horses, the first thing they wanted to do was to turn back to the stable, where they could eat and have a nice time and be comfortable. So I began to pull on the reins, and I saw that if you gave a very gentle pull before the horse could develop a desire to start turning in that direction, it wouldn't go back to the stable. Probably there are other things that I didn't know about that I could have done, but in this sort of way the horse goes where you want to go. I would say that this turning of the horse is a good analogy to the operation of the subtle intelligence on thought.

The horse, left to itself, begins to go where it wants to and develops the desire to do so. People might think that such desire is different from thought. But we can see that this is not so. Thus, the word *desire* has a root *desideratum*, meaning "what is needful." However, it means a bit more than this really. You get a sense of needing something when you desire it, but what happens typically is that you think about something that you suppose to be wonderful, and this gives rise to an image in your mind. Then the emotional function of the mind, which cannot clearly distinguish the image from reality, takes that as being real, or something just on the verge of being reached, and it tries to get there. As we were saying in earlier chapters, thought begins to make a demand. If you can't get that object immediately, the easiest way (at least momentarily) to satisfy the demand is to stir up the imagination some more. But in this way, you also build up the desire, and that creates a yet stronger urge to do something to satisfy it. Advertisers are constantly taking advantage of this. For example, they might give on television an image of somebody in a speeding car, obviously having a wonderful time, to induce you to imagine yourself to be the driver. This sort of thought develops desire all the time, and it runs away with us.

This is just like what happens with the horse. Thinking the faintest little thought about how nice it is back in the stable, it starts to turn. And as it turns, it is reminded more strongly of all these nice things in the stable. So it builds up the desire. And if you allow the horse to turn around and start to gallop, you'll never stop it from going back to the stable. You've got to stop it before it gets to that. That's the way with thought. It builds up desire, and desire runs away.

Now desire may have its place for the animal, and you obviously have to desire what is genuinely needful, but once we desire the conglomerate, memory-based image and build up this image into a conditioned reflex, the process feeds on itself and ceases to have meaning. For then, when desire is frustrated, thought can turn to creating self-deceptive images that seem for a moment to provide what is needed, and thereafter, coherence breaks down, so that the process ceases to be meaningful.

ME: Yes. It can be difficult to see the difference between the image and reality. We come back to this fundamental problem in different ways. The ability to build up images makes civilization possible, but, for the reasons that you have just given, it also contains the seeds of its own destruction.

DB: Desire originally had a useful function, and in a certain limited context, it still does. But it is now running away with itself, producing terrible confusion and conflict everywhere.

But this analogy with the horse and rider goes even further. Suppose that the horse has been jogging along rather mechanically for a long time. The rider falls asleep, and the horse begins to go where it wants to. Perhaps the rider occasionally wakes up and sees what has happened. The rider corrects the direction but falls asleep again. That's what's happening to us. We live in this rather mechanical way, doing routine work and slowly jogging through life, while the intelligence falls asleep. The "horse" runs away and develops its own direction. All the crude functions of thought begin to take over: fear, rage, anger, pleasure, and all that. We have said that there may be a kind of desire that has meaning. But the kind that we generally have are like the desires of the hired horse that are allowed to take over. You will probably end up in the stable, where you hope to get your comfortable place and your satisfying meals before you are hired out to ride again. But, as we have been saying, this sort of desire has no meaning, for it leads to boredom and a sense of deadness. And in the long run, it gives rise to a self-deceptive defense even against evidence that the continuation of the desired state of comfort and security is actually quite precarious. This whole state of mind is evidently incapable of the subtle intelligence needed to meet the inevitable uncertainties of life.

The point is, we can't properly raise the question of meaning unless this intelligence awakens. The kind of meanings we are going to get in our present state are not going to be very significant.

ME: We've been going into this question of meaning, and for me this inquiry with you has great value for my whole life. Photography and environmental problems are important to me, but it would be too limited if I just tried to show the problems in themselves, without trying to show them in a broader context as a mirror of our chaotic and fragmentary thinking. But, of course, one has to see all this in still broader contexts. For example, even the environmental movement tends to participate in the general fragmentation, because of competition for funding and attention, as well as for other reasons. Moreover, it could easily run out of steam if its whole purpose is just to restore the environment. If the scope of the endeavor is limited, then the meaning is also limited.

DB: Yes, and if this meaning is limited, the sense of purpose is limited, as well as the sense of value and the energy.

ME: And collectively, the environmental movement might break down into a lot of fragmented groups. On the surface, these might appear to work together but in actual fact do not really get on very well, running each other down and feeling a bit jealous of each other's achievements, instead of finding ways to work together.

DB: In that case the whole environmental movement could fall prey to the same illness that it is trying to cure. If the environmental movement is to be successful in attaining its objectives, it will have to pull together. What is really needed is dialogue of the kind that has been described here so that it will be able to share meanings. Otherwise, it is likely sooner or later to develop nonnegotiable differences of opinion within itself, based on different people's identification with the different assumptions with which various members come to it. If that happens, it will fall into internal conflict, and its energies will be scattered. It would be a tragedy if the environmental movement were to end up as fragmented as the world that it aims to heal. This whole movement would then lose its meaning.

ME: I certainly hope that this does not happen.

But now, let me change the subject. People often ask, What is the ultimate meaning of life? What would you say to this question?

DB: When life as a whole is harmonious, we don't have to ask for an ultimate meaning, for then life itself *is* this meaning. And if it isn't, we have to find the reason, by looking into life as a whole, which includes the source of the stream and the basic roots of consciousness and the thought process. If we do this, we will generally find that a lack of meaning in life has its root in sustained and pervasive incoherence in our thoughts, in our feelings, and in how we live, along with a self-deceptive defense of the whole process against evidence that it has serious faults.

We could say that life as a whole is grounded in the matter of the universe and also in some subtle level that we could call *spirit*, which literally means "breath or wind." We have to reach this total ground to be able to live a life that *is* its own meaning. If we take less than this sort of overall cosmic approach, the meaning we find will ultimately prove not to be a viable meaning but one that will sooner or later break down into incoherence. Whatever anybody does obtains its meaning in this overall context. And if this meaning is really coherent, there can develop a sense of value and purpose, which in turn implies interest and the arousal of energy.

ME: You are talking about having a sense of interest, which is not dependent on something in particular but is just to have that sense of self-sustaining energy.

DB: Yes. To have this sort of energy, we have to have a genuine meaning that can flow coherently into every aspect of life. Of course, this includes culture, which is, as has been pointed out earlier, a shared meaning. If you had a society that was only interested in entertainment and pleasure and utility, it would not be worth living in. The point is that, in our society, culture is being stifled, because it is turned into a commercial product through the requirement that everything has to give value for money. We now talk about the entertainment industry. We might soon be talking about the education industry, or eventually about the culture industry. The whole thing would then become a farce, because our shared cultural meanings would depend on their monetary value. We have to see that meaning is in itself the source of all value. Everything else, including money, takes its value in this context.

We have to be careful about taking too narrow a meaning, as we were saying earlier. For example, some might criticize what was said in an earlier chapter, when I pointed out that environmental work by itself can only buy time. My statement might appear to give this work too small a meaning, so that those who do it would never get the energy from that meaning to do what they have to do. To answer this, we have to come back to the idea that meaning can exist only in the whole context, in which we include also the inquiry into thought and the commitment to dialogue. It's like an enterprise in which everybody has a function, but the meaning is in the whole, not in any particular job. Buying time is one of the functions, but its significance is that it is part of this whole thing. Each person has his or her place in the whole thing.

ME: We've been saying that it is necessary to see the place of all these problems — environmental, social, political, individual, and so on — in the whole, if we are to have an overall coherent approach. But you pointed out that this whole cannot be comprehended solely in the individual and collective dimensions of the human being but must also include what you called the cosmic dimension. Would you say that without contact with this dimension, the subtle intelligence that we need to sustain coherence in life as a whole is not possible?

DB: I think that this is so. Of course, we cannot give a prescription for how to come into contact with the cosmic dimension. This requires accepting a sense of great risk in our exploration; risk is needed for the kind of creativity that is required. I would add, however, that until we at least make a good beginning in bringing about greater coherence in the individual and collective dimensions of life, our minds will be too confused and noisy to allow any significant approach to the cosmic. In an earlier chapter, I compared this situation to the lights and noise of Las Vegas, which prevent us from seeing the universe of stars. It is partly for this reason that this book has been so strongly concerned with the individual and collective dimensions. Nevertheless, it has always been implicitly pointed also at the cosmic dimension.

ME: If the mind is very noisy, then it is clear that what is required for coherence is silence. In the silence, the faint intimations of the subtle intelligence that is deeper might be sensed. So it seems that silence is essential to bring about coherence and wholeness.

DB: Yes. We may consider coming in this way upon a mind that is more and more subtle, more sensitive, more refined, more delicate, more undefinable, and more freely moving. Ultimately, it might be that this would go beyond the word, though at some stage it would come back to the word. Such a mind could move in a deeper way in the silence without the word and without the image.

A good analogy into what has just been said comes from physics, in which sound is explained as a wave in a medium such as air, which carries this wave. Even in the absence of sound, the medium is always there and is present everywhere. However, the medium is in itself silent. So the fundamental being of sound is in something that could at least metaphorically be called a deeper ground that is not sound. Similarly, thoughts can be regarded as waves or ripples on a deeper ground that is not thought. The silence of thought, that is, its nonmovement, is what is needed for us to come into contact with this deeper ground, within which the movement of thought takes place. Even when there is "noise," the ground of this is what we have metaphorically called silence. So in this sense, the silence is the deeper being, the true being, within which all the words, images, "noise," and so on can be held in wholeness. Only with such a perception can the subtle intelligence operate without impediment.

To go further into all this would take us beyond the scope of the book. Indeed, the content of this book, which is devoted mainly to the individual and collective dimensions, has to be grasped in actual life, at least to some extent, before exploring the cosmic dimension and the silence that goes with it has much meaning. We hope that the reader will actually face the challenge of doing this, and we feel that only in this way can the further challenge of changing consciousness be met fully.